# Getting in *TTouch with Your Dog*

# Also by Linda Tellington-Jones

## Books

**The Ultimate Horse Behavior and Training Book**
Enlightened and Revolutionary Solutions for the 21st Century

**The Tellington TTouch**
Caring for Animals with Heart and Hands

**Getting in TTouch with Your Puppy**
A New and Gentle Way to Harmony, Behavior, and Well-Being

**Getting in TTouch with Your Cat**
A New and Gentle Way to Harmony, Behavior, and Well-Being

**TTouch for Healthcare**
The Health Professional's Guide to Tellington TTouch

## DVDs

**Hit It Off with Your Horse!**
Understanding and Influencing Character and Personality

**Unleash Your Dog's Potential**
Getting in TTouch with Your Canine Friend

**TTouch of Magic for Dogs**

**TTouch of Magic for Cats**

**TTouch of Magic for Horses**

**Tellington TTouch for Happier, Healthier Cats**

Linda Tellington-Jones

with Gudrun Braun

# Getting in TTouch with Your Dog

## A Gentle Approach to Influencing Behavior, Health, and Performance

Translated by Christine Schwartz

TRAFALGAR SQUARE
North Pomfret, Vermont

First published in 2001 by
Trafalgar Square Books
North Pomfret, Vermont 05053

Revised in 2012 by Trafalgar Square Books

**Printed in Singapore**

Originally published in the German language as *Tellington-Training für Hunde* by
Franckh-Kosmos Verlags-GmbH & Co. KG, Stuttgart

Library of Congress Control Number: 2011940371


Photos by Gabriele Metz/Kosmos except: p. 13 (courtesy of Martina Simmerer); p. 26
(Linda Coote); pp. 28, 45 bottom, 81, 97 bottom right, 99, 101, 114, 115, 119 top, 120, 121,
125 top, 125 bottom right, 127 top left and bottom right, 128, 129 (Jodi Frediani); pp. 32,
81 bottom left and right, 105 bottom left and right, 108, 109 (André Freiling); p. 17 (Ingo
Hoffmann); p. 8 bottom (Stevie Johnson); p. 5 top (Sandra Wilson); p. 9 (Eleanor McCul-
ley); p. 23 right (Karl-Josef Rühl); p. 27 (Rema Strauss); p. 8 top (Aaron Strong); pp. 29 and
97 top right (courtesy of Robyn Hood); p. 21 (Linda Tellington-Jones).

Illustrations by Cornelia Koller

Cover design by RM Didier
Typefaces: Dolly, Strada Condensed, and Vista Sans

10 9 8 7 6 5 4 3 2 1

# Contents

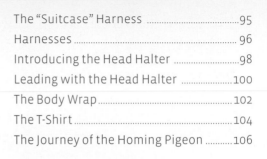

# Tellington TTouch™ Training—An Overview

## CIRCULAR TTOUCHES

The basic one-and-a-quarter circular TTouch® reduces stress and fear and enhances relaxation, awareness, intelligence and the ability to learn. The intention of the TTouch bodywork is to support and enhance cellular communication and keep your dog happy and healthy. Most of the TTouches are named after animals that Linda Tellington-Jones has worked on.

Abalone TTouch, Lying Leopard TTouch, Clouded Leopard TTouch, Raccoon TTouch, Bear TTouch, Tiger TTouch, Troika TTouch, Llama TTouch, Chimp TTouch and Coiled Python TTouch.

## TTOUCH SLIDES AND LIFTS

Strokes on the dog's body are called *slides* to differentiate TTouch from massage. The intention is to bring awareness, confidence and a sense of well-being. When doing the Lick of the Cow's Tongue or the Zigzag TTouch, your hand slides smoothly across the hair with a light contact. When using the Python TTouch *lifts* and the Inchworm, the skin is slightly lifted, which increases circulation, is relaxing and encourages deeper breathing.

Python TTouch, Tarantulas Pulling the Plow TTouch, Hair Slides, Lick of the Cow's Tongue, Noah's March, Zigzag TTouch.

## TTOUCHES ON SPECIFIC PARTS OF THE BODY

Some of the TTouches are applied to specific parts of the body, such as the ears, tail or legs. Depending on the TTouch, these can be *circles*, *lifts*, and *slides* across the hair. The Ear TTouch is useful to calm and focus and effective for bringing a dog

out of shock or preventing shock after an injury. The Mouth and Tail TTouches influence emotions, while Leg Circles improve balance and flexibility.

**Abdominal Lifts, Mouth TTouch, Ear TTouch, Leg Circles, TTouches on or with the Paws, Tail TTouch.**

## THE PLAYGROUND FOR HIGHER LEARNING®

Negotiating the obstacles in the Playground for Higher Learning teaches a dog to cooperate and concentrate, and enhances mental, physical and emotional balance. The more obstacles the dog can negotiate, the more cooperative, balanced and focused he will become. The Playground for Higher Learning is especially effective for shy, hyperactive, unfocused or reactive dogs.

**Labyrinth, Various Surfaces, Teeter-Totter, Board Walk, Cavalletti, Star, Ladder, Tires, Slalom with Cones.**

## TELLINGTON TTOUCH EQUIPMENT

The Tellington TTouch equipment has been developed over many years to enhance the effects of the TTouch bodywork and ground exercises. With the use of a variety of harnesses, leash techniques and head halters, dogs are encouraged to think and cooperate without the use of force or dominance.

The equipment has been designed and selected for just that purpose. It can bring a dog into balance and prevent pulling on the leash.

**The Wand, Balance Leash, Balance Leash Plus, Super-Balance Leash, Suitcase, Harnesses, Head Halters, Body Wraps, T-Shirt.**

# Basic Knowledge

More than a decade has passed since the first edition of *Getting in TTouch with Your Dog* was introduced to the market. Today, people in more than 30 countries use the Tellington TTouch on their dogs to educate, train, change behavior, improve performance and enhance health and well-being. Countless case studies have shown that TTouch develops a deep bond and a special connection between people and their dogs.

## Change Your Mind, Change Your Dog

One amazing result of the Tellington TTouch experience is that you will learn to see your dog with new eyes. The method inspires a partnership that far exceeds that seen in traditional training. You will develop a new awareness, a new point of view and see new possibilities for yourself and your dog.

If you are able to visualize the behavior you would like your dog to display, you can elicit that behavior without force. It is a common human habit to focus on undesirable actions: he barks, he's nervous, aggressive, afraid of loud noises, jumps up on people, or pulls on the leash. That's the behavior that sticks in your mind. You can change the undesirable behavior by holding a clear image of just how you would like your dog to behave.

When your dog jumps up on you, imagine him keeping all four paws on the ground. Imagine he moves in balance instead of pulling on the leash. See him as confident when he is nervous or afraid.

A basic premise of the Tellington Method is "By changing posture, you can influence your dog's behavior." Combining the TTouch with exercises from the Playground for Higher Learning and the Tellington Equipment, you can enhance a dog's awareness of his own body and posture. And by changing posture, you can change undesirable behavior. One example is the tail that is tucked between the hind legs—a clear sign of insecurity or fear. When the tail carriage is changed, the dog will become more confident and overcome the instinctive fear response. A variety of TTouches on the tail will enhance the dog's awareness and result in a confident attitude (see p. 31).

*This sweet Rhodesian Ridgeback, Nina, is sometimes insecure in new situations. Here she stands nicely but shows her slight insecurity with her tail against her body.*

*With one hand on the flank I circle the top of the tail mindfully to give Nina a new sense of connection to her tail and to instill confidence.*

Your thoughts can change circumstances. The well-known author and journalist Lynne McTaggart uses her book *The Intention Experiment* to teach us that creative scientists have proven how you can realize goals through the power of your intention. Have a look at her website www.theintentionexperiment. com for more information.

## What is Tellington TTouch Training?

Tellington TTouch Training for dogs is a gentle, respectful method of training honoring the body, mind and spirit of animals and their people. It has four components:

- Bodywork called the Tellington TTouch.
- Ground exercises called the Playground for Higher Learning.

*Gentle Lying Leopard TTouches on the muzzle, lips and gums are useful to calm and focus your dog due to their effect on the limbic system, the part of the brain that controls emotions.*

- Tellington Training Equipment.
- Intention: Holding positive pictures in your mind of how you want your dog to behave, perform and relate to you.

Tellington TTouch Training enhances learning, behavior, performance, health, and develops a trusting relationship between dogs and their people.

## The History of Tellington TTouch

Tellington TTouch Training for dogs evolved from my work with horses, which over the decades has expanded to include all animals as well as humans.

Doing bodywork on animals is generally thought to be a modern trend. However, my grandfather Will Caywood learned a form of equine massage from Russian gypsies that was the cornerstone of my interest in bodywork for animals. In 1905 while training racehorses at the Moscow Hippodrome in Russia he was awarded the title of Leading Trainer of the Year for producing 87 winning horses that season. He received a prize of a jeweled cane from Czar Nicolas II. My grandfather attributed his success to the fact that all horses in his stable were "rubbed" over every inch of their bodies for thirty minutes each day with this gypsy massage.

In 1965, my then husband Wentworth Tellington and I wrote a book entitled *Massage and Physical Therapy for the Athletic Horse* based on the Russian gypsy massage. We used this system of massage on our horses for recovery after 100-mile endurance competitions, steeplechases, three-day events, and horse shows—all of which I competed in extensively. We found that our horses recovered much more quickly with bodywork.

However, at that time it never crossed my mind that the behavior and character of an animal, and its willingness and ability to learn, could be influenced by bodywork. That all changed in 1975 when I enrolled at the Humanistic Psychology Institute in San Francisco in a four-year professional training taught by Dr. Moshe Feldenkrais, the creator of a brilliant system of mind-body integration for humans.

My enrollment in this four-year course was an unlikely move on my part as the Feldenkrais Method was developed for the human nervous system, and I came from the world of horses. I had been teaching riding and training horses for over twenty years at that time, and for the past ten years had co-owned and directed the Pacific Coast Equestrian Research Farm and School of Horsemanship, dedicated to the education of riding instructors and horse trainers.

I signed up for this training thinking I could use the Feldenkrais Method to enhance the balance and athletic ability of my riding students. I was driven by an intense, intuitive "feeling," which for some inexplicable reason prompted me to take this course. It's almost as if I "knew" that the Feldenkrais Method, known for increasing athletic ability, alleviating pain, and improving neurological dysfunction whether it be from injury, illness or birth, would become exceptionally effective in improving the performance and well-being of horses.

In July, 1975, I had an "ah-ha" experience that lead me to the development of a new method for training horses. It occurred as I was lying on the classroom floor with sixty-three fellow students following the instructions of Moshe Feldenkrais. This was only our second day of the training and we were being guided through a series of gentle movements called Awareness through Movement®. Moshe made the statement that a human's potential for learning could be enhanced, and learning time shortened dramatically, with the use of non-habitual movements. These movements could be done sitting, standing, or lying down and consisted of exercises that bring new awareness and function to the body.

It was the theory of Moshe Feldenkrais that these non-habitual movements activate unused neural pathways to the brain, and awaken new brain cells, thereby increasing one's ability to learn.

Whey I heard this statement, my first thought was, "What movements could I do with a horse that will be 'non-habitual,' and could increase a horse's ability to learn?"

From 1975 to 1979 I spent summers in San Francisco in the Feldenkrais training and the winters in Germany working on countless horses developing a method of non-habitual movements over a variety of obstacles. By working through The Labyrinth, The Star, and Platform horses made remarkable improvements in behavior and balance and demonstrated a new willingness, and ability to learn without pressure or force. (These obstacles are now known as The Playground for Higher Learning, and dogs that can negotiate these and other obstacles become more cooperative, balanced and focused.)

With the encouragement of Ursula Bruns, founder of the Reken Test Center in Germany, and the support of my brilliant sister, Robyn Hood, a system evolved that was originally called Tellington Equine Awareness Method or TTEAM. The work is now known as the Tellington Method and Tellington TTouch Training.

## The Birth of the Tellington TTouch

In 1983, my focus shifted from the Feldenkrais Method to the exploration of the magical Tellington TTouch Circles. The Tellington TTouch was birthed as a result of an "epiphany"—defined as "a sudden intuitive leap of understanding, especially through an ordinary but striking occurrence." This "sudden occurrence" happened at the Delaware Equine Veterinary Clinic in July of 1983. I was working with a twelve-year old Thoroughbred mare that was in much pain and would normally attempt to kick or bite when groomed or saddled. When I put my hands on her she became very quiet and her owner Wendy could hardly believe her eyes. When she asked me, "Why is my mare so quiet? What is your secret? Are you using energy? What are you doing?" without thinking, I intuitively replied, "Don't worry about what I'm doing, just put your hands on the mare's shoulder, and move the skin in a circle." I was surprised at my reply, but I had learned to trust my intuition so I waited to see what would happen. Moving the skin in a circle was not something I had consciously done before. I watched in amazement as Wendy made small circles on the shoulder and the mare stood as quietly for Wendy as she had for me.

It was in that moment that I realized something very special had happened. Over the ensuing months and years, I experimented with various pressures, sizes, and speeds of doing the circles. I used my hands intuitively in many different ways, responding to what the animals liked. My sister, Robyn Hood, who is as observant as an owl, has worked with me over the years to clarify the techniques of this method.

*Stroking with the wand can calm and focus a dog.*

*This black Labrador is very excited and tense, and his head carriage is reflecting his emotional state.*

## Cellular Communication

A primary intention of Tellington TTouch is to enhance cellular communication and support the healing potential of the body. My interest in cells was awakened in 1976 while reading the book *Man on His Nature* by the British Nobel Laureate, Sir Charles Sherrington. I had a second life-changing experience when I read the statement, "If several inches of a nerve are removed, most of the time, the two ends will find their way back together. How is this possible? Because every cell in the body knows its function within the body, as well as its function in the universe." This is how I remember the quote for Sherrington.

I was awestruck by the intelligence of the 50 trillion cells that form the average body, and the fact that every cell can function on its own and yet display remarkable cooperation and communication with other cells when a person or animal is healthy and in a state of well-being

I began to see the body as a collection of cells and was struck with the concept that by touching another body, I could allow the cells in my fingers to convey a simple message of support at the cellular level: "Remember your potential for perfect function; remember your perfection...." This is a primary message that is carried in each Tellington TTouch Circle.

When asked how it's possible to have such a deep connection and trust with animals I've never met before—in such a short time—I'm convinced it is because I connect at the cellular level. Tellington TTouch is an interspecies language without words.

## Tellington TTouch Today

Today there are more than two dozen TTouches each one having a slightly different effect on an animal. As I discovered more TTouches I realized we needed names for them, not just ordinary names, but unusual, creative names that would be easily remembered. It seemed natural to name the TTouches for different animals I had worked on, the ones that evoked special memories.

For instance, the inspiration for the name the Clouded Leopard TTouch came from my work with a three-month-old leopard at the Los Angeles Zoo. She had been rejected by her mother and had developed the neurotic habits of sucking her leg, and kneading her paws, for hours on end. I did small circles on her mouth to address her emotional issues, and on her paws to help relax them and bring more feeling. The "cloud" part of the name describes the lightness with which the whole hand contacts the body (as lightly as a cloud), and the "leopard" stands for the range of pressure of the fingers. A leopard can be very light on its feet as in the light TTouch, or very strong as in the higher pressure TTouches.

The Python TTouch was named for Joyce, an eleven-foot-long Burmese Python that I worked on for a demonstration at the twentieth annual Zoo Keepers Conference sponsored by the San Diego Zoo in California, in 1987. Joyce suffered from recurring pneumonia every spring. When I first started to work on her using tiny Raccoon TTouch circles, she was twitchy and didn't like it, so I intuitively switched to doing slow, small lifts under her body to stimulate her lungs. After a few minutes Joyce stretched out to her full length, and I let her go for a "slither" to get some exercise. When I resumed working on her with small circles again, she relaxed completely and turned to watch me with her nose almost touching my hand.

TTouch builds confidence, instills cooperation, and develops an animal's ability and willingness and ability to learn. It takes animals beyond instinct, teaching them to think instead of react. It is a system based on gentle circular movements, lifts, and slides done over every inch of an animal's body. The intent of the TTouch is to activate the function of cells and enhance cellular communication. You can liken it to "turning on the electric lights of the body." TTouch is

To win trust I perform connected Clouded Leopard TTouches on the dog's forehead while my other hand is stabilizing his head.

The Python TTouch brings awareness and new sensations to a dog's legs, which helps a fearful and nervous animal by making him more "grounded."

done over the whole body, and each circular TTouch is complete within itself. It is not necessary to understand anatomy in order to successfully change undesirable habits or behavior or speed up the healing of injuries or ailments

TTouch can release pain and fear. When I began to see major changes in traumatized animals that I was working with twenty years ago, there was little understanding, and no research to explain the results of TTouch. Neuroscientist, Candice Pert, in her book, *Molecules of Emotion*, has now proven that emotions are held in our cells and transported to our brain by neurotransmitters. I believe that is why the TTouch has had such success in releasing fear and bringing a new sense of confidence and well-being to animals and their people.

For three decades thousands of people have reported success using Tellington TTouch despite having no previous experience with the method. We now have studies that show that TTouch affects stress hormones and lowers pulse and respiration in

nervous humans and animals. Studies by teach, author and researcher Anna Wise have shown that the circular TTouch activates the whole brain in a special pattern called the "Awakened Mind State" in people doing TTouch or receiving TTouch. This is the brain-wave pattern of highly creative people and healers and may explain why so many people working with the Tellington Method have so much success.

## Tellington TTouch Training for Dogs

World-renowned scientist Rupert Sheldrake, in his fascinating book *Dogs that Know When Their Owners Are Coming Home*, demonstrates that dogs can read our minds and pick up our mental pictures even when far away. It confirms to me that it was the clarity of my expectations that made my dogs so cooperative over the years, and that this is the difference between success and failure in so many cases of inappropriate behavior.

on the dog's ability to learn. The limbic system is responsible for:

- Self-preservation as well as preservation of the species
- Emotion and feeling (excitement and fear)
- Fight and flight response
- Memory storage

It is involved with:

- Respiration
- Heart regulation
- Feeling pain
- Feeling temperature change
- Smell and sight
- Regulating fluids
- Body temperature
- Circulation
- Intake of nutrition

## Stress

Depending on the reasons, and its intensity, all living beings respond to stress in different ways:

- Fight
- Flight
- Freeze
- Faint
- Fidgeting and chewing

Many changes in behavior—and ailments—seen in dogs have been caused by stress. When we have a better understanding of the source of their stress and how it affects them, we have more tools to help dogs deal with it.

### "Calming Signals"
Careful observation is the key to understanding the communication signals our dogs give us. When dogs feel threatened in a particular environment or situation, it is even more critical to recognize and respond to these signals to avoid triggering confrontation or undue stress. Turid Rugaas has described many behaviors that dogs use to convey information to other animals and to humans, which she terms "calming signals." Turid defines these signals as "the language of peace, which enables dogs to avoid and solve conflicts and live together in a peaceful manner." Some of the more frequent calming signals you may observe include:

- Yawning
- Licking
- Turning away/turning of the head
- Play bow
- Sniffing the ground
- Walking slowly
- Moving in an arch on approach
- Sitting down and lifting a paw
- Scratching

Just as we don't continuously stare at people when we approach them or invade their "personal space," dogs and other animals also give signals to define their personal space or comfort level. It is highly desirable that dogs both give and recognize these signals to cope appropriately in social situations. It is also important for people to recognize calming signals and be aware that these communication signals can progress to stress signals, particularly if the signal is initially ignored or there is continued threat. We can use body language and calming signals ourselves to convey non-threatening intent and build trust when working with dogs who exhibit signs of stress and/or extreme behavior responses. Averting our eyes, approaching from the side, kneeling down, speaking in a soft

*Licking his lips is sometimes a "calming signal" that dogs use to show a need to settle a difficult situation.*

*What is going on over there? This dog displays tense muscles with a posture that makes it difficult for him to listen to his handler.*

voice, and using the back of our hand upon initial contact are all ways in which we can signal to the dog that we are indeed "listening" to their concerns.

From a TTouch perspective, you also look closely at posture and balance. When a dog is out of balance physically, he is often out of balance emotionally and/or mentally. Posture gives you many clues about a dog's physiological state of arousal and state of concern in a particular environment. Tail tucked, ears back, mouth drawn tight, and head lowered is often a posture seen with dogs that are in a state of fear or anxiety. Head up, tail relaxed, equal weight on all four legs with ears forward is a posture you may observe in a dog that feels calm and confident. Signs of stress:

- Increased respiration
- Shaking
- Tight muscles
- Restlessness
- Vocalizing (barking, whining, howling)
- Fooling around (e.g. tail chasing)
- Excessive grooming (e.g. genitals and paws)
- Increased irritability
- Chewing objects
- Excessive licking
- Drooling
- Extreme tail wagging
- Refusing to accept treats
- Inability to concentrate
- Sweaty paws
- Shedding

Digestive problems, loss of appetite, diarrhea or urination problems are also common signs of stress. In the case of chronic stress, you can often notice an unpleasant body or breath odor, a dull hair coat showing dandruff, itchiness and scratching.

## What Happens in a Stressful Situation?

During a stressful situation, hormones are flooded with adrenalin and cortisol to prepare the body for flight or fight and it takes the dog's body a long time after the threat has gone to recover. You can speed this up considerably with the use of TTouch, the Body Wrap and the Ground Exercises. Stroking the animal with a Wand can also help reduce stress, especially if used in the earliest stages of a stress-inducing situation.

# Posture During Stress

"Change the posture, change the behavior." Dogs show their emotions very clearly in their posture. A dog that is afraid may show it by tucking his tail between his legs. When you are able to change his posture, you can also change his behavior.

## SIGNS OF STRESS:

| | |
|---|---|
| **Mouth:** | • Lips pulled back<br>• Drooling<br>• Dry<br>• Stiff lips<br>• Puffed-up cheeks |
| **Ears:** | • Erect<br>• Held tight to the body<br>• Pulled back<br>• Folded |
| **Eyes:** | • Wide open<br>• Staring<br>• Seeing the white of the eye<br>• Squinting |
| **Head carriage:** | • Too high<br>• Too low |
| **Tail:** | • Stiff<br>• Between the legs<br>• Tense and close to the body<br>• Excessive wagging |
| **Body posture:** | • Crouching<br>• Rolling onto back<br>• Tense upright posture<br>• Very still |
| **Breathing:** | • Excessive panting<br>• Holding breath |

## A Vet's Point of View

*Martina Simmerer, a veterinarian who has a veterinary practice for holistic veterinary medicine in Austria, has been using The Tellington TTouch Method for many years. She has been involved with the Tellington TTouch in depth since 1987 and TTouch for dogs and horses has been an integral part of her practice and seminar activities for fifteen years.*

Dr. Simmerer writes:

"I had just started Veterinary School when I first heard about the Tellington TTouch Method. The reason why I took my first class was because of a problem horse that did not respond to any conventional method of treatment. When I found out how quickly I was able to help that horse with the Tellington TTouch, I was totally fascinated. I realized right away that I had finally found the method of working with animals that I had been searching for years.

"However, I was trained in the sciences, and hence skeptical. I have to test a new approach in order to see whether it really is as valuable as it seems at first sight. While I was a student I was taught to question everything and to observe carefully. Consequently, I documented my progress with my first study group and kept a detailed TTouch training diary. Later, when I had more experience, I started a TTouch work group with my students at the Veterinary School. The University of Vienna has always been blessed with open-minded professors. For example, acupuncture has been taught there for many years, and in 1989 and 1990, Linda Tellington-Jones was a visiting professor at the Department of Orthopedics. That department also hired me in 1998 to teach an elective course called Bodywork for Rehabilitation and Behavior Modification. Twenty-four students completed the course."

*Austrian veterinarian Martina Simmerer has had very good experiences with the Tellington TTouch and uses it daily in her practice.*

### Is the Effect of TTouch Measurable?

"To scientifically prove the effectiveness of the TTouch, Linda Tellington-Jones supported several studies measuring pulse, brainwave patterns and blood cortisol levels. All the results indicated that the TTouch elicits changes in the animal's body. An elevated pulse can quickly be lowered when the animal is treated with TTouch Bodywork. Brainwave-pattern measurements showed increased brainwave activity, which is typical when learning takes place. Blood tests showed that stress hormones lessen when the animal is TTouched. Extensive scientific measurements and analyses are not yet published. As soon as my veterinary practice allows me more time I will set up a study on the effects of TTouch on the cortisol levels in stressed animals. A German biologist is currently working on a study of how TTouch treatments affect the pain level in humans.

"At this point we have only been able to observe that TTouch lessens the stress level, reduces pain and creates a calmer, more relaxed and compliant animal, but more scientific studies are underway."

### One of Countless Examples

"When Linda started to develop her work with dogs, the veterinarians who were already involved with TTEAM for horses were immediately supportive. All of us have to deal with far too many dogs shaking in fear on the examination table, or having to be dragged into the exam room. If we can im-

*When a dog starts to rest his head like this, it is a sign that he trusts the person.*

prove the animal's experience at the vet clinic even a little bit it not only helps us but the animal and his owner.

"I will never forget our first dog training. One colleague brought her Husky who would not allow anyone but her owner to touch her. It took her boyfriend two years for the dog to barely tolerate him. On the first day the Husky hid under the table, showing a lot of fear. Trixi, one of the practitioners, stroked the dog with a Wand, then turned it around and made TTouch circles with the button end. Slowly, she was able to slide her hand up the Wand and sneak in a few very quick TTouch circles with the back of her hand. This session lasted maybe ten minutes when Trixi felt the dog had enough and gave her a break.

"When we sat together at the end of the day discussing what we had learned, the Husky came out of her hiding place, sat beside Trixi, placed her head on Trixi's thigh, and allowed herself to be petted. We were blown away and could not imagine that she could have changed so quickly. Experience has taught me that results are not always that fast—usually, a bit more time, knowledge and patience are needed—but the results are there, nonetheless, especially when compared to traditional training methods."

Use of the TTouches in a Vet's Practice
Martina Simmerer continues:

"You should always be aware that your safety is most important. A dog in pain can snap, or bite, by reflex at any given moment even if he is usually extremely mellow. This is why in a potentially dangerous situation you should use a muzzle, or have another person restrain the dog safely. It often happens that people concentrate so hard on doing TTouches that they forget to pay attention to their own body language. You should avoid any gesture or body position that may seem threatening. For example, do not lean over a dog or stare one directly in the eye.

- "To make contact with a nervous animal use random, one-second Clouded Leopard TTouches. This allows you to gain a dog's trust and makes the examination easier.
- "If there are areas on a dog's body that he won't let you touch or treat, use the Raccoon and Clouded Leopard TTouches in connected lines.
- "The TTouch not only helps an animal 'release' his fear and tension, but it is also an excellent aid for treating pain. Injury

healing can be accelerated with the TTouch; wounds heal a lot faster, comparable to a successful laser treatment. However, hands are always 'at hand' and are a lot less expensive than complicated machines. Wounds must, of course, be cleaned, disinfected, and often sutured and bandaged. After this has been done perform Raccoon or Lying Leopard TTouches with extremely gentle pressure around and on the bandaged area.

- "Animals with arthritis, spondylitis, or degenerative hip disease respond well to supportive TTouch treatments. The diagnosis of incurable joint disease is very frustrating to a veterinarian and, especially, to a dog's owner. With the TTouches, an owner can be empowered to alleviate his or her dog's pain and to minimize the use of drugs.

- "Properly performed, the Tail TTouch helps with problems in the spine and the intervertebral disks.

- "For dogs of large, fast-growing breeds that tend to have problems with growth and coordination, the TTouches can improve the connection from the front to the back of the body. The Zigzag TTouch, Tarantulas Pulling the Plow, and Connected Circles, are all especially helpful.

- "Many dogs suffer from recurrent tooth and gum diseases, such as plaque, tartar, inflamed gums, and even cavities. Good preventive care includes a special diet and regular tooth brushing, which is a lot easier if the animal is used to the Mouth TTouch.

- "You will quickly win over the heart of a dog by gently massaging the animal's ears. This is one of Linda Tellington-Jones' most important discoveries. The Ear TTouch should be a regular part of

the veterinary repertoire because it can save a life. It is extremely useful in a case of shock after an accident, in circulatory failure, in heatstroke, after anesthesia as well as in a case of fright from less dramatic situations, such as carsickness."

*The Mouth TTouch is important in a veterinary practice as it prepares the dog for a stress-free examination of teeth and gums.*

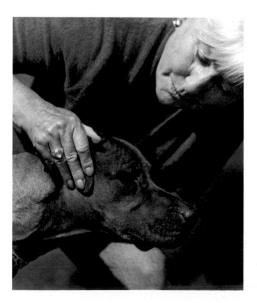

*The Ear TTouch can save a dog's life in case of shock.*

## Leading Exercises and Groundwork in a Vet's Practice

Dr. Simmerer goes on:

"Veterinarians are often asked questions about animal behavior. The ground exercises with 'non-habitual' movements (the Feldenkrais concept described in the introduction to this book) enhance an animal's physical and emotional balance. This work greatly improves concentration and coordination, and changes the learned behavior patterns of animals as well as humans. The goal of the ground exercises is to bring the dog's body into balance, and to provide the animal with an enjoyable and stress-free experience of his own body. Eventually, the dog will be able to act consciously rather than react instinctively.

- "An excellent aid to solving many problems is the correct use of the Holt (formerly known as the Halti) or a similar head halter (p. 98). We always use the Holt in combination with a flat collar (not a choke chain, or choke collar), or a harness, in order to avoid any damage to the dog's cervical vertebrae. It is a well-known fact that the conventional method of 'correction,' a jerk on a choke chain, can seriously damage a dog's neck and larynx.
- "The Body Wrap gives fearful and hyperactive dogs a subtle framework, and helps them feel more secure. Child psychologists use similar 'wrapping' techniques to treat panic attacks, for example."

## The Experience of a Dog Trainer

*Stevie Avastu is a behavior consultant and dog trainer in Great Britain. She is famous for her success with aggression, and other behavioral problems. Many dogs of various breeds are trained for Schutzhund (protection) work by using wrong methods, so are not reliable around people. Often Stevie is the last resort for such dogs, their owners and trainers. She writes:*

*A head halter combined with a regular flat collar or harness helps to bring the dog back into his own balance.*

# Tips from Veterinarian Daniela Zurr

Daniela Zurr is a German veterinarian, Tellington TTouch Practitioner for dogs, and author of two books in German about the Tellington TTouch in a veterinary practice and holistic behavior therapy for dogs (and cats). She has put together a list of the TTouches she has found most useful in her practice.

| | |
|---|---|
| **Ear TTouch** | "After anesthesia and surgery, the Ear TTouch helps to stabilize the cardiovascular system. If the dog is restless, we place him in a warm and quiet area and stroke the ears slowly and gently. If his ears are cold and he is having a difficult time waking up, stroke faster and more vigorously." |
| **Belly Lifts** | "Belly lifts can bring a lot of relief to a dog with a digestive upset or stomachache. When his belly is very tight, use very light lifts. When the touch of your hand is too much for the dog, use an elastic bandage to perform very small, gentle lifts." |
| **Mouth TTouch** | "We know from human medicine that gentle stimulation of the face results in relaxation. You can TTouch your dog's mouth to reduce stress or help him deal with too much excitement." |
| **Clouded Leopard TTouch** | "The bladder meridian runs along the dog's back muscles parallel to the spine. This meridian covers all the important acupuncture points that deal with the animal's organs. Therefore, TTouches along the dog's back supports not only the back muscles, but also the function of his organs." |
| **TTouch on the Paws** | "Have you ever noticed how lightly and effortlessly a dog moves over rough terrain? Or that he rarely steps into excrement left behind by another dog? The paws are covered with countless sensitive nerve endings; this means that you need to pay special attention to the paws and teach your dog that he can trust you to handle them." |
| **Tail TTouch** | "A dog who has had his tail docked often shows a lot of tension in the stump area and this affects his balance and way of going. When this tension is released, the dog's movement improves dramatically. Luckily, most dogs now get to keep this important part of their body, but even dogs with unaltered tails can suffer from back pain and fear, which can create tension in their tail area. The Tail TTouch helps to create hind-end awareness and confidence." |
| **Llama TTouch** | "This is my favorite TTouch when I make a first connection with an animal, and is great when working in an animal shelter—or just when meeting any new dog. When a dog is unsure, it is important to combine the Llama TTouch with your body language: Look away from him, turn your body away, and take deep breaths." |

*Several dogs working together on the Playground for Higher Learning. Walking over low Cavalletti motivates the dogs and their owners.*

"I first learned about the Tellington TTouch Method in the early 90's from participating in a weekend workshop. I found the ideas interesting, but also a little 'crazy,' and did not try them myself. In the summer of 1996, I found out that Linda Tellington-Jones was going to give a class in my area, so I decided to take it. When the day was over, I was fascinated by what I had seen and learned. Linda's demonstration kindled my interest and motivated me to finally try the TTouch work. Since then I have taken advantage of every opportunity to learn more about it.

"Many dogs with all kinds of issues are presented to me. Some are like a whirling dervish, others are shy, and others aggressive. The common denominator in most of these cases is stress. Stress prevents an animal from learning new lessons. This is the reason why the calming effect of the

TTouches is so useful. Again and again, I find that a twenty-minute session of the TTouches suffices to relax a dog's tense body. Tension gives way to calmness and receptivity, and the dog becomes more attentive.

"As stress diminishes, the dog's self-confidence increases. The dog is now able to change unwanted behavior patterns. When the dog's owner performs bodywork on the animal, the relationship between the two of them improves. This is a very important step toward success because I am only a mediator, it is the owner, after all, who has to take the dog home and teach him new behaviors.

"The ground exercises are extremely valuable in various ways. The dog learns to pay attention to different tasks. Fear is 're-leased' as the dog learns to concentrate on a specific exercise. His coordination and rhythm improve, which is very important

*Doing TTouches with others in a group can be very helpful for the dog that behaves inappropriately around others.*

for competition and agility training. In addition, the groundwork helps to balance the dog, which means that he learns to stand and sit in his own balance without pulling, or leaning, into a person. In other words, the dog learns to take responsibility for his own behavior. This is the key to dealing with behavioral issues."

## Katja Krauss

*Katja Krauss is a dog trainer and author living in Berlin, Germany, also a Tellington TTouch Practitioner. She writes:*

"For me the Tellington Touch is a method with unlimited possibilities. It is practical, easy to learn and helpful in all types and levels of dog training. It is much easier for a puppy to 'learn how to learn' when his train-

ing is supported with TTouch. Fearful or overly rambunctious youngsters often settle immediately when you have them wear the T-Shirt (p. 104).

"Overly needy dogs can learn a new way of relating to people through the non-habitual movements of the Playground for Higher Learning (p. 109). I am still amazed how quickly dogs change, and would not believe it possible if I had not seen it happen hundreds of times.

"Dogs that take part in agility and obedience events, regular conformation shows, as well as dogs involved with rescue, service and the police, can all benefit from TTouch. They show an improved attention span, better posture and coordination after receiving a TTouch session and prior to entering the show ring or starting their duty. I use it all the time with my own dog who is trained to find mold in buildings. Dogs that visit the elderly or sick learn how to enjoy being handled, and assistance dogs connect more quickly with their owner and benefit from the TTouch's relaxing release of tension.

"The Tellington Touch is complimentary to other training methods, such as clicker training. It is known all over the world. I have even received an invitation to demonstrate TTouch at the palace in Dubai.

"TTouch practitioners and affiliates stay connected through Internet chat groups, and new ideas are constantly exchanged to keep the method ever growing and evolving. New Leading Positions and more detailed TTouches are added to the curriculum to keep making the work more effective and easier to teach.

"TTouch is not very spectacular to watch, but the results give the method the credit it deserves. In my opinion, this is the present and future way of dealing with animals."

## Bibi Degn and Elia

*Bibi Degn is a Tellington TTouch instructor and head of the TTouch Guild in Germany. She writes:*

"Can you imagine bringing home a dog from Malta who lived by foraging in the streets and then finding out later she is pregnant? To make matters more difficult, she delivers eleven bouncy pups.

"One of those puppies is Elia, born in my third-story apartment in Germany. She turned out to be just the dog I needed. Elia is happy, she can wag her tail up and down, right and left and in a circle in both directions. Well, she can do that today—but she could not when I first met her.

"Back then she would tip her head to the side and look at me in an adorable way that told me she had absolutely no idea what people were about and what they wanted from her. The street dogs of Malta are not just called 'street dogs' because that is where they live. It is a specific breed that has learned through generations to live near humans and steal some food, but also to be fiercely independent and very careful not to get caught.

"Elia tried hard and learned. This was not an easy task for her. Everything a good street dog needed was deeply imbedded in her. Food was her number-one priority; she was afraid of strangers, terrified of children and had an incredible hunting instinct. I had been teaching for years that TTouch and positive reinforcement would help most behavior problems, but Elia needed a lot more help than any other dog I had ever been with, and required many more TTouches. She made me think!

"It was time to test my own theory. What I really wanted was a dog who would accompany me on horseback rides through the forest—off-leash and problem-free. Linda thought I should give up and put her on a leash because a dog like Elia could not be loose in a forest. The challenge was on!

"Elia taught me how much TTouch can assist in willingness to cooperate. Now I have a wonderful dog who gives me endless joy. She accompanies me on long on rides—not a leash in sight; she amazes me with her speed and agility as she jumps and leaps over sticks and stones. She returns to me at my softest call, even when a deer is crossing a few feet ahead on the path.

"We learned together without my having to yell at her even once, or ever having to use any type of negative reinforcement. I am terribly proud of us. Elia—the challenge—

*Bibi Degn and Elia. Bibi has been the head of the German TTouch Guild for many years.*

*Bibi is also the editor of the German quarterly TTEAM Newsletter, which is packed full of interesting articles and case studies.*

has been a great success and I can now say with 100-percent conviction that even when working with very difficult dogs, if you know what you want and know the TTouch, you can achieve a level of cooperation that you could have never imagined."

## Karin Petra Freiling and Schampus

*Karin Petra Freiling is a biologist, an instructor and the organizer for the "TTouch for You Trainings" in Germany. She writes:*

"Schampus is a testament to the magic of the Ear TTouch: Two years ago, a horse suddenly kicked out and hit his head. Schampus was thrown twelve feet and when he landed, blood flowed from his ears and nose. He was unconscious when I picked him up and the bridge of his nose was fractured. Linda's words, 'When there is an emergency, work the ears right away,' popped into my head, and I immediately started to stroke his ears from the base to the tip.

"A few moments later Schampus came to and a friend drove us to the vet clinic while I kept working his ears. When I stopped for a

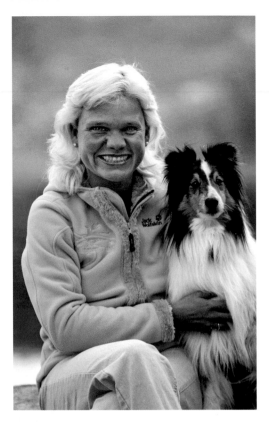

*Karin Petra Freiling, shown here with Chablis, is a biologist and Tellington TTouch Instructor for Companion Animals and Humans (TTouch for You, the Tellington TTouch Method for Humans).*

*Karin and Schampus whose life was saved by the Ear TTouch. Karin is a naturopath and active in animal rescue.*

few moments to give him some Rescue Remedy, he lost consciousness again, his body tensed and he suffered an epileptic seizure. I went back to working the ears immediately and he regained consciousness.

"The veterinarian gave him an injection to reduce the swelling on his nose but did not give us a lot of hope. He said there was a lot of trauma to the brain and we needed to be prepared for the worst: the chance of Schampus surviving the night was extremely slim.

"I took Schampus home and my husband Andre and I spent the entire night taking turns TTouching his ears. We never stopped because every time we took a break, he lost consciousness.

"Luckily our beloved dog not only survived the night, he made a full recovery. Today, Schampus is my loyal and professional companion. He accompanies me to demonstrations about TTouch and loves 'doggy dancing.' Words cannot express how grateful I am that I knew about TTouch at the time of his accident."

## Gabi Maue and Tiber

*Gabi Maue is a Tellington TTouch Practitioner 3 for Companion Animals in Germany. She writes:*

"I have always searched for a gentle, respectful way to train animals and since my first two dogs were easy and uncomplicated, I never had to enroll them in classes or therapy sessions.

"This all changed when our third puppy, Tiber, came into our life. He was extremely fearful and we had no idea why. However, when he was two years old, the vet diagnosed the beginning of a genetic eye problem. By the time he was three, Tiber was blind. This shattered his world: He became extremely insecure, would only stand up if there was a wall to lean against, and when we took him outside, stayed glued to our side. If we tried to lift a paw, he would bite. We now realized that Tiber must have had problems with his vision when he was a puppy—we just did not recognize it at the time.

"We adopted a three-year-old bitch, Fanny, to be his companion, but unfortunately, she turned out to be a fear biter toward people as well as dogs. Right at that time Linda Tellington-Jones was scheduled to do a demonstration in Aachen, Germany about TTouch for dogs.

"I was thrilled to see how quickly she

*Gabi Maue with Quiviv du Pas du Loup, her five-year-old Pyrenean Shepherd dog who has become a valued assistant in Gabi's clinics.*

*Through TTouch, Tiber has become a calm, cool and collected dog in spite of his blindness. Here, Gabi and Tiber are attending a dog show.*

achieved changes in the dogs there by using a method that shone with calmness, gentle touching, no hint of aggression, dominance or pressure. This was exactly what I had been searching for.

"My dogs were equally thrilled and loved the TTouch. However, I became restless and felt a strong need to share this incredible knowledge with other dog owners and their animals. In 1998 I enrolled to become a TTouch practitioner for dogs.

"I have taught clinics, hands-on workshops and individual clients, and for the past five years have been working with the largest dog-training organization evaluating unusual dog behavior and seeing how TTouch can help.

"TTouch has changed my life in so many different ways and I am grateful to Linda for the work she does for all of us."

## Lisa Leicht and Golfy

*Lisa Leicht is a Tellington TTouch Practitioner 3 for Companion Animals, and she resides in Bern, Switzerland, and Cavaliere, France. She says:*

"My personal TTouch success story started thirteen years ago. At the time I was living in the country and my five-month-old Jack Russell's favorite pastime was chasing mice with my cat. The fun ended when, after eating the mice, she consistently suffered from severe stomach pains lasting for days, which stunted her growth and development.

"As a solution to keep her from getting sick, my veterinarian suggested putting a muzzle on Golfy when she went outside. For me, this was not an acceptable option, so the search for an alternative began.

"A friend told me about an American woman who 'pulled dogs' ears' to bring them back into balance. By coincidence there was a clinic being held nearby, and having nothing to lose, I signed up.

"The work fascinated me right away. I loved the respect and awareness Linda showed the animals and wanted this method to be part of my life. I was an eager student and soon making circles on Golfy's ears, stroking them, performing Belly Lifts, and wrapping her up in a Body Wrap.

"Golfy was receptive, enjoyed the bodywork, and I had the sense that the connection between us strengthened during the

*Lisa Leicht with Durga the stuffed dog, an ever-patient and obedient model when it comes to fitting different TTouch equipment.*

*Lisa and I are leading the poodle Giacomo in Journey of the Homing Pigeon. It is important when taking the dog through the Playground for Higher Learning to always stay level with the dog's shoulder.*

weekend. I continued using the TTouches after the weekend and a few days later, it became clear that my little dog had no problem digesting mice.

"That sealed the deal for me: I was so grateful for the wonderful gift that I immediately signed up for the three-year education course to become a TTouch Practitioner. I was so thrilled that I would be able to partake in the well-being of my own animals and those I came across. Today I am a Level 3 Practitioner

and lucky to be able to share this amazing work with many dogs and their owners.

"Golfy is now an elderly lady, but she insists on coming along when I teach workshops and watches from her basket to make sure everything is in order. She demands her daily TTouch session to help strengthen her and keep her feeling well. She still enjoys going through the Playground for Higher Learning, which helps her to maintain her concentration and some coordination in her old age. TTouch is a wonderful tool for me to be able to thank my dogs for their patience, adulation and cooperation."

## Debby Potts and Shawna

*Debby Potts is a Tellington TTouch Instructor for Companion Animals and Horses, and she lives near Portland, Oregon. She writes:*

"One of the personal passions that I offer with TTouch is the idea of teaching dogs life skills, not just obedience commands. Many

*Debby Potts is using the TTouch on Kiki. Debby teaches trainings in the United States and many other parts of the world. You can see her on the DVD Unleash Your Dog's Potential showing how to use the Body Wrap.*

dogs are very good at obedience but when they are off a command, their behavior can be so disruptive that it can cause trouble in a family. Shawna was a five-year-old Giant Schnauzer who threatened the relationships in her human family. Her constant whining was so disturbing that Robert, the husband, wondered if he could continue to live in the house with Shawna. He and his wife Joan joined a dog-training club and tried many different approaches to stop Shawna's whining, but nothing helped. In desperation, they brought Shawna to me for a private session.

"In checking her body I found that her cropped ears were extremely tight. It was almost as if they were cemented to her head. I worked with TTouches all over her body and went back to her ears several times, allowing time in between for the information from TTouch to be processed in her cells. By the end of the session, Shawna's ears had released their tension and were actually longer.

"A basic philosophy of TTouch states that 'changing the posture changes the behavior.' It was certainly true for Shawna. Just relaxing her ears and releasing the tension in her head made a marked difference. 'Change your mind and change your dog,' is another principle of the Tellington Method. I encouraged Shawna's people to imagine her being quiet and calm and as a result of TTouch—and, I believe, changed expectations on their part—the whining stopped. I think of it as the session where I helped a dog and saved a marriage."

*Kathy Cascade is working on a clinic dog that is being introduced to a head halter. She is using TTouches as a reward for a job well done on the Playground for Higher Learning.*

## Kathy Cascade and Alf

*Kathy Cascade is a TTouch Instructor for dogs. She works with rescue dogs and lives in Oregon. She writes:*

"In the course of our TTouch work, we sometimes encounter animals that have suffered various forms of neglect, abuse, or violence—often at the hands of humans. It is difficult not to be overwhelmed or angered by these sad stories, but it's more important to focus on the animal before us in the present moment. Our intention when working with these animals is to help them move beyond the limitations of their past experiences to reach their full potential."

After being rescued from a dog-fighting compound and spending some time with

a rescue group, Alf and his foster guardian, Molly Gibb, worked with Kathy.

"When Molly and Alf arrived for their first visit," Kathy reports, "Alf cowered on the floor of the car and would not get out. No amount of coaxing or offer of yummy treats worked—Alf just would not budge! Of course, we could have pulled him or lifted him out of the car, but that would have defeated the goal of giving Alf some choice and earning his trust."

Finally, Kathy's dog, Indie, coaxed Alf out of the car by walking back and forth past the open car door for a few minutes.

Alf was extremely fearful, and the first few sessions involved taking tiny steps to build his trust one experience at a time. Kathy introduced Alf to the Body Wrap to start reducing his "bracing" pattern and touch sensitivity. She says, "The initial sessions were brief, and I allowed Alf to move away as needed. Giving him some choice seemed to lessen his fear and eventually he started to approach me, staying close to be TTouched for longer periods of time. Our goal was to introduce Alf to several safe new sensory experiences, allowing him to gain confidence."

The impact of Kathy's work with Alf was apparent a few months later, when Molly brought a transformed Alf to one of Kathy's weekend workshops. Kathy joyfully reports, "Alf handled the situation beautifully! Witnessing Alf's newfound confidence and ability to cope with so many different people in an unfamiliar environment was a profound moment for both Molly and me."

## Edie Jane Eaton and Arlo

*Edie Jane Eaton is an Instructor for dogs and horses and lives near Ottawa, Canada. She says:*

*Edie Jane Eaton has been a TTouch Practitioner for many years and teaches clinics in North America, Europe, South Africa, New Zealand, and Australia.*

"Arlo was a young Great Dane, regal and long-legged. His posture made him appear a few inches smaller than he really was. His owner, Nancy, brought Arlo to a clinic hoping he could overcome his shyness and change his habitual pattern of urinating in the garage when he was afraid.

"I noticed Arlo's low head carriage right away, as well as his clamped tail, lack of interest in his surroundings and the need to lean against Nancy. He had to be close to Nancy and leaned against her as soon as she took a step to the side. Leaning is often seen as a sign of affection, but it is more accurate to see it as lack of mental balance and confidence.

"It was impossible to lift Arlo's legs to do Leg Circles. I wondered if this lack of balance would also show up when he was walked on a leash, and yes, he was a puller. I suspected that Arlo's balance was the trigger for his urination problem. He only felt safe in the garage—the place he dared to stand on three legs.

"Arlo also had a dry mouth, cold and stiff paws, a very tight tail and the tendency to hold his breath. That gave us lots of areas to work on to help him find his balance and overcome his shyness. We tried a bit of everything in my TTouch tool box, starting with the Playground for Higher Learning where I walked him with the Balance Leash. I noticed right away that he would lose his rhythm when asked to walk slowly.

"Python Lifts on the legs helped increase circulation and 'grounded' him. These worked wonders for Arlo as did Chimp TTouches on his paws and mouth. I wet my hands before I worked inside his very dry mouth, and used the Tail TTouch to improve his posture and change his self-image.

"We placed a Half Wrap on Arlo to

encourage him to breathe deeper and increase his flexibility. The Balance Leash taught him to shift his balance onto all four legs. Abalone TTouches on his shoulders and belly, as well as very gentle traction on his tail, also helped to change his posture. We used the Journey of the Homing Pigeon to give him a sense of his space.

"When we were finished Arlo looked like a new dog. His head and tail were held high and he was able to look around. Arlo no longer leaned against his person but stood well-balanced on all four paws. Leg Circles became easy and effortless and he no longer pulled on the leash.

"And, much to his owner's delight he stopped urinating in the garage."

## Robyn Hood and Roy

*Robyn Hood, Instructor for dogs and horses, lives at her Icelandic Horse Farm in Vernon, British Columbia, Canada. She writes:*

"It sounds crazy that a large, strong Belgian Shepherd who effortlessly runs up and down steep hills and dashes through mud and uneven terrain cannot master going up some stairs in the house. But this was my dog Roy's problem.

"He had always been kept outside before he came to live with me. He could go up and down stairs that were open on the sides but not those going up or down with walls on either side. The bedrooms were upstairs and he was very motivated to go up there, but frightened to do so.

"I started by putting on a Body Wrap and just asking him to come near the bottom step. I did some Ear Strokes, Zigzags and Abalone TTouches on his body. I sat on the

*Robyn Hood with her Belgian Shepherd, Roy. Robyn is my sister and the cofounder of Tellington TTouch Training. Robyn teaches clinics all over the world and is the editor of TTEAM Connection.*

stairs and offered him a bit of food on the floor in front of the step, then he took a bit of food from the step. I asked him to come closer by stroking the leash. He put one foot onto the first step, and then his other front foot. I gave him a few treats off the next step, then just let him stand there for a few moments. At that point I moved him away from the stairs and said 'That's enough,' and left it at that.

"Within a couple of hours he was walking up the stairs on his own. Instead of making a big deal of the steps I just gave him a 'taste' of what was possible, let him think about it, and it was like he took a breath and thought he could do it."

# The Tellington TTouch

The Tellington TTouch is a gentle form of bodywork consisting of circles, lifts and slides done with the hands all over the body. The second "T" in TTouch stands for "trust." TTouch has been described as an interspecies language without words. You will experience a magical connection when you TTouch your dog. I will guide you through the different TTouches on the following pages.

## How Does TTouch Bodywork Affect the Dog?

TTouch is a non-verbal language that deepens your connection with your dog. Just a few minutes of TTouch a day can create amazing positive results in your dog's confidence, attitude, personality and behavior—and support his health.

The goal of the TTouch bodywork is to activate the life force and function of cells and awaken their intelligence, which creates physical and mental balance. More trust is created between you as your dog gains self confidence.

TTouch stimulates the body's ability to heal itself and also the ability to learn. Neurologist Anna Wise worked with the psychobiologist and biophysicist Maxwell Cade, who discovered that a consistent pattern of alpha, beta, theta and delta waves were apparent in both hemispheres of the brain when a person was in the most effective state of mental functioning. Cade called this the "Awakened Mind State."

Anna discovered that when doing one-and-a-quarter TTouch circles, all four of these brain-wave patterns are stimulated in the human, which sets the ideal state for learning. Even more remarkably, it was shown that the people doing the TTouches—as well as the ones being worked on—exhibited the same distinct brain-wave patterns.

Further studies with Anna using horses showed the same activation of all four brain-wave patterns in both hemispheres of the brain in the animals that were receiving TTouch. And, in 1985, a study done by Russian veterinarians at the Bitsa Olympic Equestrian Center in Moscow showed a reduction in stress-hormone levels in horses as they received TTouch. You can find more information about these scientific studies on my website (www.ttouch.com). Watch my DVD *Unleash Your Dog's Potential*, and you will see how different dogs respond to TTouch bodywork.

### TTouch Supports Intelligence

Webster's definition of intelligence is "the ability to adapt to new situations." TTouch can be very helpful in teaching animals to adapt to new and potentially stressful environments.

Just like people, animals find themselves stressed from time to time. TTouch is a wonderful tool to limit the negative effects of stress and transfer the animal into a state of relaxation, promote an "openness" and ability to learn, and absorb the situation. This state will help the dog and his handler deal

*The Tellington TTouch helps me make a trusting and respectful first contact with this dog.*

with something new or difficult without fear or concern.

With the help of TTouch you can cement a strong bond with your dog that is built on trust. A dog who trusts you will go through fire for you!

Through TTouch your dog will receive more awareness of his body and he will feel more confident. The TTouches help reduce fear, nervousness and tension. Some of these may look like massage, but they are very different from massage. The pressure is very light and the movements have a very specific effect on the cells. I like to refer to it as "turning on the lights"—the goal being to enhance the potential for healing in each cell in the body.

## The Nine Elements of TTouch

There are nine important elements in Tellington TTouch Training. Become familiar with them and you will find success.

### 1. The Basic Circle
The hand does not slide over the skin but instead, "moves the skin" over muscle. Imagine the face of a clock drawn onto the skin. Start at six o'clock (the bottom) and move the skin clockwise once around the circle and then on farther to nine o'clock (the left side of the clock). This creates a one-and-a-quarter circle, which is the basic TTouch circle. You should usually work clockwise. However, be mindful of the direction: if your dog does not like it clockwise, first try going counter-clockwise, before changing your pressure, speed, or trying a different TTouch.

### 2. The Pressure Scale
TTouch pressure is rated on a scale from

*TTouch allows this dog to be more comfortable in her body and supports her emotional and physical balance.*

Numbers 1 to 10, however when working with dogs you should only use Numbers 1 to 4. Start with a Number 1 pressure, which is the lightest possible contact. Remember that your main goal is to support cellular function and communication.

#### • Pressure 1
To get a sense of these pressures, support your bent elbow with one hand, and with the other, rest your thumb on your cheek and use your fingers to gently move the delicate skin below your eye in one-and-a-quarter circles. Be careful not to slide your finger across the skin. Repeat the same circle on your arm and notice that there is almost no indentation in your skin with a Number 1 pressure.

• Pressure 3

To feel the Number 3 pressure, move your fingers about an inch lower to your cheekbone. Allow the weight of your curved middle finger pad to connect clearly with your cheekbone and feel a circle there. Repeat the same pressure in a circle on your arm and observe the indentation in your skin. Notice the difference between Number 1 and 3 pressures. The Number 2 pressure is between 1 and 3.

**Helpful hint:** Find the pressure that feels right to you and your dog. When you are working with an injury or inflammation use less pressure: Numbers 1 or 2 are enough. Number 3 is a very common pressure. Once you are more familiar with the TTouch, you will know instinctively the pressures that are best for any given situation.

## 3. Tempo

The tempo is the time it takes to move the skin around the circle-and-a-quarter. We use one to three seconds. To *activate* a dog use the one-second circles, and when you want to *settle him* or *bring focus*, use two-second circles. One-second circles are most effective for reducing swelling and relieving

acute pain. Remember: When you want to stimulate the dog, use faster circles, and when you want to settle him, slow the circles down.

## 4. A Mindful Pause

After making several circles on the body, hold the connection at the end of the one-and-a-quarter circle with a momentary pause. We playfully refer to this with the acronym P.A.W.S. meaning, "A Pause that Allows a Wondrous Stillness." This gives the dog time to integrate the new feeling.

## 5. Connecting the TTouches

The TTouches are done all over the dog's body. Rather than randomly skipping from area to area, it can be better to work in lines with a gentle slide of the fingers from TTouch to TTouch—generally from front to back. However, when working on painful, sensitive or injured areas, do not connect the circles. Instead lift your fingers off the body and make a smooth move through air to connect again gently before the next circle. We call this "weaving."

## 6. Body Position

Your dog can be standing, sitting or lying down. Make sure that you are in a comfortable position so you can apply TTouch in a relaxed manner. When TTouching a small dog it's more comfortable having the dog on a table or on the sofa with you.

With the dog on the ground, find a comfortable and safe position. If the dog is nervous, or you don't know him (a shelter dog, for example), for safety, avoid leaning over him. If you are working with a fearful or reactive dog sit on a stool or a chair so that you are balanced and can move away easily.

Use both hands when you are TTouching

an animal—one hand for TTouch while the other connects and contains the dog.

When working on the head or ears support the dog with one hand under his jaw. When working on his back it is helpful to have your other hand supporting his chest or TTouching the same area on the other side of his body.

### 7. Mindful Breathing

It is a common human trait to hold your breath when you concentrate. Inhaling

through your nose and exhaling slowly through pursed lips will keep you calm, focused and energized from the oxygenating effect of this conscious breathing. This form of breathing is called PEEP (Positive

End Expiratory Pressure). Observe how this breathing will also influence your dog's breathing and keep him calm and relaxed.

## 8. Intention

A primary intention of TTouch is to hold a positive image of how you would like your dog to behave, perform, and relate to you, knowing that you can influence behavior and health by the intention you hold.

I live in Hawaii where I learned from a spiritual leader about an exercise called "Pono and Pilikia." *Pono* means means a state of perfection, an ideal state of being. *Pilikia* means trauma or drama, and in our useage represents the issues or behavior you would like to change.

Pono and Pilikia can help you change the behavior of your dog. It's such a common human trait to only see the issues or problems our dogs have, sometimes forgetting the positive aspects. When a dog's behavior is out of control it can be very frustrating so write down your thoughts to help you realize the gifts your dog brings to your life.

In a few cases this exercise has helped to clarify that a dog is not suitable for the family, or for the job for which he is intended. In most cases, the dog's owner realizes that the problems are not as serious as she had thought and is relieved that she could find a solution with Tellington TTouch.

Take a sheet of paper and draw a perpendicular line down the middle. At the top of the left side and under the word *Pono* list everything you love about your dog. On the right, write *Pilikia* and list all the dog's undesirable behaviors you would like to change or improve.

## 9. Feedback

Since your dog can't use words, listen to his language and watch for the smallest signals. Take note of any "calming," vocalizing, avoidance or physical signals your dog may be exhibiting. To start you need to learn your dog's signs for:

· Fear and shyness

---

**Success Secret 1**
**Look at your dog's behavior or health not in the way your eyes see it, but the way you would like it to be!**

Pretend that your wishes have already come true. Feel the emotion that you would feel if you had already reached your goal. Let the feeling of joy flow through your body and celebrate with your perfect, healthy dog. Your dog's behavior is linked to:

Your **expectations**
Your **posture**
Your **clarity**
Your **reactions**
Your **guidance**

Keep the picture of the perfect dog in your heart and your thoughts. This will open a door for your dog to become just the way you want him to be.

## Success Secret 2
### Remember your dog as perfect.

Once you have developed the habit of repeating "my dog is perfect," to yourself, you will convey to him how wonderful it is to see him so "perfect," and your connection together will flourish and grow.

An old saying, "Sow an action for twenty-one days and you will harvest a habit," is very appropriate in this case. When you repeat something for twenty-one days it will become "yours," and you can do it without thinking.

Look for small steps of improvement and focus on these. You will then notice how everything falls into place.

- Hyperactivity, being overly sensitive
- Lack of focus
- Being inflexible, blocked learning
- Aggression

Other signals that your dog is not comfortable are:
- Holding his breath
- Freezing
- Tucking his tail between his legs
- Twitching
- Restlessness
- Any signs of insecurity or tension

You should acknowledge these signs by TTouching your dog on a different spot or changing the TTouch, pressure or speed to show him that he can trust you and that you are willing to listen to his concerns.

## Safety Tips

- If you are not a professional dog trainer or TTouch Practitioner it is safer to work with your own animal only.
- When TTouching your own dog, you should know him well and not be afraid of any potential sudden defensive move. Always be careful.
- Never look a frightened or aggressive dog straight into the eye. This can be perceived as a threat to some dogs. Do, however, keep his face in your peripheral vision, with your eyes remaining soft and friendly.
- Approach the dog from the side and start TTouches on his shoulder.
- Be aware of feedback from the dog. Reduce the pressure, change to a different TTouch or move to a different area when the dog seems nervous or concerned.
- Many dogs like to lie down during a session, but some prefer to stand or sit. Make sure you are comfortable, keep your wrist straight and be mindful of your breathing.
- Support the dog's chin while working on his head or ears. When working with a dog that has a sore back or hips, contain the dog's chest with your other hand while you are TTouching the tail or back.
- To contain a small dog that is jumping up or turning around, slide your thumb under the collar with the rest of your hand containing the chest.

# Builds trust and instills comfort

# The Abalone TTouch

Because the contact with your whole hand provides warmth and security, this TTouch is ideal for sensitive dogs. You can also help nervous animals calm down and relax. Dogs who are very sensitive to being touched or brushed can overcome their fear and resistance with the help of the Abalone TTouch.

## HOW TO

To do the Abalone TTouch, place your hand lightly on the dog's body. Your whole hand moves the skin in the basic one-and-a-quarter circle. It is important that you use just enough pressure so that your hand does not slide over the surface of the skin but actually moves it. The Abalone is very similar to the Lying Leopard TTouch (p. 40), but since the whole hand moves the skin in a circle (instead of the fingers), it is easier to do.

Your other hand establishes a connection and softly supports the body. The typical tempo for the Abalone TTouch is two seconds and it is always done with very light pressure. If the dog is in pain, use a Number 1 pressure; if there is tension, use Number 1 or 2 pressures.

After finishing the circle connect to the next circle by sliding your hand along the body before starting it.

Make a mindful pause after three or four TTouches to give the nervous system the time to integrate the TTouches.

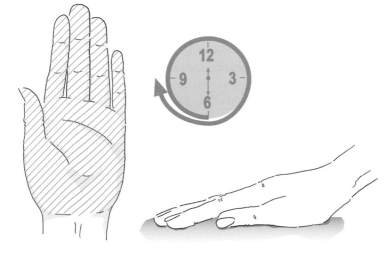

## WHAT IT LOOKS LIKE

**1 Chest** The Abalone TTouch is great for calming nervous dogs and for relaxing tense and painful muscles in a dog's chest. The warmth of the hand contributes greatly to this effect.

**2 Head and Mouth** Abalone TTouches on the side of the head prepares the dog for TTouch on the Mouth. Calming Abalone TTouches on both sides of the head creates a quiet connection and a sense of trust. In the photo, I am gently supporting the muzzle between my two hands to calm and create trust.

**3 Back and Ribs** Slow, soft Abalone TTouches with a Number 2 pressure and two-second circles along the back and ribs relax Nina enough so she lies down and closes her eyes. I'm using the Abalone TTouches in connected lines along her ribs.

### What should you do if..
#### ...your dog won't stand still for TTouch?

You may need to gently contain a nervous, shy or young dog in the beginning. If your dog is quiet to start with but starts to get restless or wants to leave after you have begun the TTouches, there are several possible solutions:

- Adjust your pressure and speed.
- Be aware of your breathing, and relax.
- Soften your fingers.
- Spread the TTouches over the entire body.
- Focus on the roundness of the circle.
- Be sure the area is not sensitive or painful.
- Try a different TTouch.
- Visualize a relaxed dog.
- Keep the session short.
- Start with faster circles (one second) and gradually work more slowly.

# The Lying Leopard TTouch

The area of contact for the Lying Leopard TTouch is the fingers. This may include all three sections of the fingers or only a part of them. Although the palm of your hand will have a light contact with the body when the circles are on the body, the palm does move the skin. If you are TTouching the leg of a small dog, only the first sections of your fingers move the skin. This TTouch is designed to build trust and relaxation, and works well as a bridge between the Abalone TTouch that provides warmth and security, and the focused, precise Clouded Leopard TTouch.

### HOW TO

Put your hand lightly on the dog's body and move the skin with the underside of your fingers in the basic circle as shown in the drawing. Shaded areas of the hand are normally in contact when you are on the body, but in some cases (when TTouching your dog's head or a leg, for example) the palm of your hand is not in contact.

Your second hand contains the body as shown in the photos on the next page, and the thumb maintains a connection with the other fingers but does not make the circle.

Two-second circles calm and bring awareness. When you are finished with one circle connect it to the next one by sliding to the next position a few inches away.

After several TTouches, hold the mindful pause at the nine o'clock position to give your dog the opportunity to experience the TTouches fully.

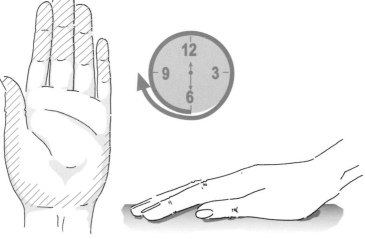

# WHAT IT LOOKS LIKE

**1–2 Head and Neck** Many dogs enjoy having their heads touched with such mindful contact. However, if your dog is independent or timid you may have to begin on the shoulders to first gain acceptance. Build his trust with gentle Lying Leopard TTouches on his forehead, on the sides of his mouth, under his muzzle, and on his neck.

**3 Shoulders** Tension in the shoulder muscles will restrict your dog's stride as well as his breathing. With these gentle TTouches you can relax tight shoulder muscles and reduce fear, nervousness, and hyperactivity, and achieve better mental, physical and emotional balance

**4 Thighs and Legs** You can help a dog with hip dysplasia or tired muscles after intense training, as well as a dog who is reactive to loud noises, by doing Lying Leopard TTouches on the outside and the inside of the thighs. Start at the top of the thigh and do Lying Leopard TTouches in lines of connected circles all the way down to the paws. Pause for two seconds at nine o'clock at the end of several circles.

# The Clouded Leopard TTouch

The Clouded Leopard TTouch is the basic TTouch. All the other Circular TTouches are variations on the Clouded Leopard TTouch. To perform this TTouch your fingers should be slightly curved with their pads lightly together. Depending on the size of your dog, you can apply a very light (Number 1 pressure) or a Number 3 on a large dog. With regular work your dog will develop more trust and willingness to cooperate. This TTouch has proven especially effective for nervous and anxious dogs. It can also help dogs feel more confident in new and challenging situations such as obedience training or competition.

The Clouded Leopard also improves the coordination in dogs that are insecure or ones that have neurological issues.

## HOW TO

Place your hand (with your fingers slightly curved) on your dog's body. Keep your fingers lightly together and move the skin around in a one-and-a-quarter circle. The darkened areas of the fingers as shown in this drawing should be in contact with your dog's skin.

Your thumb rests on the dog's body and establishes a connection with your other fingers. Keep your wrist as straight and flexible as possible. Your fingers, hand, arm, and shoulders should be relaxed. Put your other hand on your dog's body as well; this will help you maintain your balance.

The most common length of time taken for this TTouch is two seconds with Number 2 or 3 pressures. After finishing a Clouded Leopard TTouch connect it to the next by sliding across the hair, imagining the line you are following. This improves the dog's awareness of his body. Add a pause after three or four TTouches to help the dog integrate the work.

## WHAT IT LOOKS LIKE

**1 Head to Tail** When you do Clouded Leopard TTouches all over your dog's body you will make him more aware of it, as well as enhance his feeling of well-being. Begin at the center of the head and do Connected TTouches in a straight line across the neck, shoulders, and along the back. Continue with similar lines of Connected TTouches parallel to each other.

**2–3 Front and Back Legs** Tense, anxious, or shy dogs can gain self-confidence through TTouches on their legs. They also become more connected to the ground. If your dog allows it, start high up on his leg and work your way down to his paws. Your dog can be standing or sitting, whichever is most comfortable. When TTouching the paws, use a Number 2 pressure.

# The Raccoon TTouch

The Raccoon TTouch is the smallest and finest of the TTouches. It is especially useful for the most sensitive areas of the body, and it speeds up the healing process.

Use it on small body parts such as the dog's toes, and for injuries or arthritis. The Raccoon TTouch is often used on puppies or smaller breeds. You can reduce pain or sensitive areas in a very short period of time with this TTouch when you work with a very light pressure. It will speed up healing and bring more awareness to the affected area.

## HOW TO

Bend the tips of your fingers at a 60-to-90 degree angle depending on the length of your fingernails. This TTouch is applied with the tip of your finger, right behind the nail. Draw tiny one-and-a-quarter circles with a light pressure—a Number 1 or 2.

Your thumb is a connection that keeps your circles round and your pressure light.

The Raccoon TTouch is one of the faster TTouches, usually taking about one second although slowing down to a two-second TTouch can be useful to support healing. On an acute injury, use a Number 1 pressure all around the area, or you can use a Number 1 pressure Lying Leopard TTouch instead.

There are situations where even the support of the thumb is too much for the dog. With these dogs we keep the hand as relaxed as possible and avoid using the thumb. Sometimes we use only one or two fingers and if you are working in the mouth of a small puppy, your finger can be replaced with a wet cotton swab.

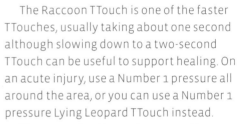

## WHAT IT LOOKS LIKE

**1 Back, Hips and Thighs**  I recommend very light Raccoon TTouches along both sides of the spine for pain or tension in the back. A few minutes a day of Number 1 pressure, two-second Raccoon TTouches on the hips have kept dogs with hip dysplasia sound for years. Some dogs develop a habit of favoring an injured leg even after it has healed. You can often reeducate the nervous system by using Raccoon TTouches to release the memory and expectation of the pain at a cellular level, and increase the dog's awareness that the leg is now healed and is safe to put his weight on it.

**2 Lower Back and Hips**  Older dogs can suffer from swelling and hardening of the lower back (loins) and hips above the kidneys. Using very light Raccoon TTouches helps to bring awareness to the area and reduce the swelling. It is important to work with the lightest TTouch because the improvement will not come from the pressure of the TTouch but from the increased awareness and activation of the healing potential of the cells. Combine the Raccoon TTouch with the Lying Leopard TTouch.

**3 Tail**  In this picture, I am making very light Raccoon TTouches on a docked tail. Amputated tails and legs can cause lifelong phantom pain. You can erase such memories and eliminate a feeling of insecurity by touching the end of the stump with many tiny, very light circles. Docked tails are often very tense and the Raccoon TTouch can ease this tension. You can also gently hold the other side of the tail with your thumb to make a connection between your fingers and thumb.

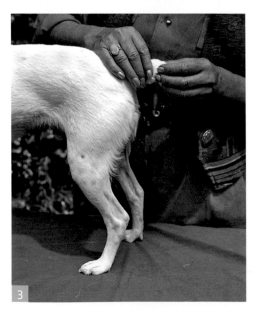

# The Bear TTouch

The Raccoon and the Bear TTouch are very similar. The difference is that your fingernails are used in the Bear TTouch, making it ideal for itchy dogs or those very heavily muscled.

## HOW TO

With the first joints of your fingers, press straight down into the skin. Make your one-and-a-quarter circle mainly with your finger-nails. If you are working on a heavily muscled area, roll the skin with your nails and finger-tips over the muscle and make a tiny circle. Hold your fingers close together. In order to do the Bear TTouch effectively, your finger-nails should be of medium length, some-where between one-eighth and one-quarter-of-an-inch. Try the Bear TTouch on yourself first to see how much you can feel your nails. The pressure should vary between Numbers 1 and 4. You may want to place a damp, cool cloth over an irritated and itchy area and do the Bear TTouch through the cloth. Apply only slight pressure—Numbers 1 to 3— on insect bites, areas of skin allergies, and hot spots.

# What should you do if...
## ...your dog won't remain sitting or lying down?

Keep your dog still by stabilizing him on his shoulders or using his collar. Focus on applying perfectly round circles and a consistent speed and pressure. Try a few circles counterclockwise, which some animals find more relaxing. However, after he settles down you should return to clockwise circles. Movement can settle the dog, so you may want to take him for a short walk or go through the Labyrinth and use some TTouches while there (see p. 114).

## WHAT IT LOOKS LIKE

**1 Head** Here you see a light variety of the Bear TTouch. I am keeping my fingers slightly apart and using all four fingers at the same time on the dog's head. Use very light pressure, work slowly and use all your fingers in the same rhythm. Also be careful that the weight of your hand isn't adding pressure.

**2 Shoulders** When working on well-muscled shoulders I keep my fingers closer together. The Bear TTouch increases the body awareness and circulation.

**3 Pelvis** The Bear TTouch can be helpful with itchiness or swelling. Start with a light Number 1 pressure and if the dog likes it, increase the pressure.

# The Tiger TTouch

The Tiger TTouch is very useful for relieving itch and soothing hot spots. It can be helpful for getting the attention of hyperactive dogs and bringing awareness to dogs with thick hair who may not feel other TTouches. Tiger TTouch has also been very effective for increasing awareness of paralyzed dogs during rehabilitation. Numbers 1 and 2 pressures are most effective.

## HOW TO

For the Tiger TTouch hold your hand upright with your fingers at 90 degrees from the dog's body with your fingernails making contact. Spread your fingers approximately one-half inches apart to stop itching or to cover a large area for increased feeling and awareness in heavily muscled or big dogs. Your thumb is held still to steady the movement of your fingers. As always keep a connection with your other hand placed on the dog's body for balance and containment.

## WHAT IT LOOKS LIKE

If your dog is excited or restless begin on the shoulders and make three or four circles with a one-second tempo. Then slow down to two-second Tiger TTouches—with mindful pauses between circles—to instill a sense of calm. On itchy areas and hot spots make two-second circles using a light pressure that is acceptable to your dog. If the hot spot is irritated or open, place a clean cloth over the area and do the TTouches through it.

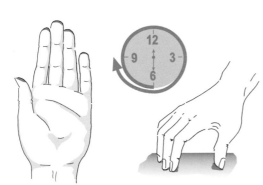

# The Troika TTouch

The Troika TTouch is one of our newer TTouches and it is considered a combined TTouch. It's a lovely way to connect with your dog with the lightest Number 1 pressure Tiger TTouch with the fingernails. I call this variation the "Intriguing TTouch." Depending on the combination it can be done to invigorate—or relax. It can stimulate the circulatory system or be calming. If you want to practice this TTouch, try it on a friend.

## HOW TO

To relax, start with the familiar, basic Clouded Leopard circle. When you get to nine o'clock, slide your fingers in a generous arc (as you might do if you played the harp moving from one string to another) in a three-quarter circle across the skin without moving the skin. Since you are making an arc you will end at a different place, so continue the next Troika TTouch from there.

When you use the Lying Leopard circle with the Troika TTouch, the result is calming. On the other hand, when you use the Tiger TTouch with the Troika TTouch, it is invigorating to the animal or "intriguing" so he wants more. It works wonders when you want to "wake up" an animal—or end a session in a quiet way.

Most dogs love the Troika TTouch, but I do not recommend it for ones with tension or pain in their back or other areas of the body. For shy or nervous dogs use the slow, light TTouches or explore the "Intriguing Tiger TTouches."

## WHAT IT LOOKS LIKE

Back   Start the Troika TTouch on the back of the neck and work along the spine toward the tail. You can get the attention of an excited or hyperactive dog by working quickly at first and then slowing the TTouches down. You can also use the Troika to re-energize your dog after a relaxing TTouch session. My dog Rayne loves the lightest possible "Intriguing Tiger TTouches."

# The Llama TTouch

The Llama TTouch is performed with the back of the fingers. Sensitive, fearful dogs perceive the touch of the back of the hand as less threatening. With dogs like these, use this TTouch at first. Once they begin to trust you, you can use other TTouches.

## HOW TO

For the Llama TTouch use the back of your hand, or fingers, to make the one-and-a-quarter circle. The pressure is always light. It can be applied using the knuckles only, or with the entire hand. As usual, start at six o'clock, and push the skin around in a one-and-a-quarter circle.

The Llama TTouch can also be used with the side of your hand. This is a good way to make a first contact with an unfamiliar or nervous dog. This TTouch is also useful for people whose fingers are not very flexible.

## WHAT IT LOOKS LIKE

1–4 Neck and Back  In these photos, I am using the Llama TTouch with the back of my fingers while my left hand is resting on the dog's back and not doing any TTouches. My contact is very light, yet firm enough to be able to move the skin in a circle.

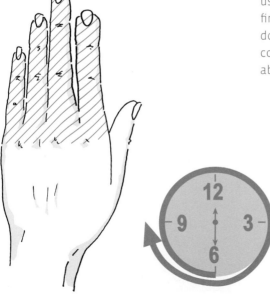

## What should you do if...
### ...your dog refuses to be TTouched?

The Llama TTouch is often appropriate for such cases. Many dogs are afraid that "open hands" are going to grab them, so it's a good idea to first touch a fearful dog with the back of your hand. This is much less threatening, and many nervous dogs then readily accept a soft touch.

# The Chimp TTouch

The Chimp TTouch is similar to the Llama TTouch and can be used to make a first connection with a dog because it promotes trust. It is also a helpful TTouch to use when your dog is in a position where it's difficult to reach him with an open hand.

## HOW TO

Bend your fingers toward the palm of your hand and use the flat part between the first and second finger joints of the back of your hand. If you are working on a puppy or really small dog, adjust the TTouch and use the back of the fingers up to the first joint as shown in the drawing on the right. Draw a one-and-one-quarter circle with the back of your fingers. You will notice that when you are using this "Baby" Chimp TTouch your fingers have more mobility and the connection to the animal is softer.

Try the Chimp TTouch on yourself at first using a Number 3 pressure.

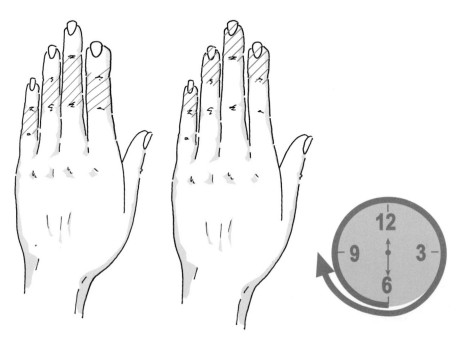

## WHAT IT LOOKS LIKE

**1 Head to Mouth** The Chimp TTouch is very useful when a dog is sensitive about having his head and mouth touched. Start at the dog's neck and connect the Chimp TTouches working toward the head and mouth.

**2 Hips** Most fearful dogs are very tense in their back and hindquarters and can be reactive to open hand TTouches. Be aware of your breathing and start with connected Chimp TTouches using a Number 1 pressure on the shoulder, carefully working your way toward the hip. Sore areas, such as an arthritic hip, can be treated with one-finger Chimp TTouches, which most dogs first allow, and then enjoy.

**3 The Orangutan TTouch** The Orangutan TTouch adds another layer of softness and awareness. It is a combination of the Chimp and Baby Chimp TTouches and you use the back of your fingertips up to the second

### What should you do if...
...your dog does not like being TTouched on his hindquarters?

Continue on a different spot carefully observing your dog's reaction and check for "calming signals" from him. Start at the neck and work toward the tail. Use a much lighter pressure than before and do the TTouch more slowly. It is possible that the dog is experiencing pain in his hindquarters, or he is afraid. Therefore, it is advisable to try a different TTouch first, (Llama TTouch, for example) or carefully stroke the dog with a Wand. You can also use the button end of the Wand to make small circles on his hind end until the dog feels more comfortable.

finger joint. Your fingers are lightly bent and your wrist is level with your arm.

# The Python TTouch

The Python TTouch is especially useful with shy, tense, hyperactive or uncoordinated dogs. Fear, tension and hyperactivity limit the dog's awareness of his body and his ability to use himself properly. The Python TTouches help him become more "grounded," which promotes mental, emotional and physical balance.

Python TTouch can also have a soothing and relaxing effect that increases circulation and reduces tension. This can be wonderful for older dogs or those with painful areas. The warmth of your hand is an added benefit with this TTouch.

## HOW TO

Place your flat hand on the body. Gently and slowly move the skin and muscle upward. Breathe with the movement and hold for a few seconds. With your other hand, hold your dog by his collar, or hold and stabilize him on his chest. Without changing the contact or pressure, slowly return the skin to the start-ing point. If you spend twice as much time releasing the skin as lifting it, the relaxing effect will be greater. When you perform Python TTouches on the legs, slide down about one-half inch after each lift until you reach the paws. When working on the body, do the Python TTouches in equal distances and in parallel lines.

## What should you do if...
### ...the dog is displaying stress signals?

Fearful, aggressive and hyperactive dogs are in a state of stress and they usually have cold and sensitive paws. Consequentially, awareness of their feet is compromised and they become insecure. Python TTouches give a dog a sense of connection to the ground, and a sense of security. For dogs competing in sport and for working dogs, the Python TTouch improves performance and reduces the buildup of lactic acid. This TTouch also improves agility, mobility, balance and evenness of gait.

## WHAT IT LOOKS LIKE

You can perform Python TTouches on the shoulders, back, abdomen and legs. The pictures demonstrate how to do them on a dog's legs.

**1 Front Legs**  Approach your dog from the side and place your whole hand around the leg just below the elbow. When you are working with a large dog you can use both hands; with a small dog you can use just your fingers. After the first Python TTouch, slide your hands down and begin again. Continue in this manner until you reach the paws if it is acceptable to the dog.

**2 Upper Part of the Hind Legs**  Encircle the thigh with your flat hands, placing your thumbs on the outside of the thigh, or place one hand on the inside and one on the outside of the leg. For safety, only bend over a dog if you know him well and are sure that he will not snap or bite. Python TTouches in this area are especially helpful for dogs afraid of loud noises.

**3 Lower Part of the Hind Legs**  Since the diameter of the lower part of the back legs is much smaller you can encircle it with both hands—or just one hand. Do the Python TTouch in whichever way is most comfortable for you and your dog. When you have reached the paws and are finished with the leg, do Noah's March on the entire leg from top to bottom (p. 64).

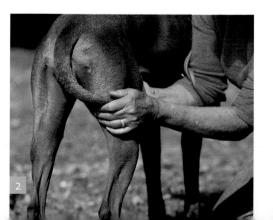

# The Coiled Python TTouch

This TTouch is a combination of the circular TTouch and the Python TTouch. The circular TTouches awaken the dog's focus. By following up with a Python TTouch the animal and handler are encouraged to breathe deeper and enter a state of relaxed attention.

## HOW TO

Use a basic TTouch circle, such as the Lying Leopard TTouch, and move the skin around the clock from six o'clock once around past six o'clock to nine o'clock. At this point, rather than releasing it, move the skin straight upward—without stretching it. Pause and gently bring the skin back downward to six o'clock.

Between TTouches on the body, slide lightly across the hair to the next circular TTouch. Feel the connection between the circles. The more mindful you are with these connecting slides, the more success you will have at giving your dog a sense of balance, focus and awareness. Do the circles and slides in lines parallel to the spine and make perpendicular lines down the legs.

When TTouching the legs, start at the top of the leg and work your way down to the paw. Do light Python TTouches on a large dog placing the thumb on one side of the leg, and the fingers wrapped lightly around the other side. After the "lift," lightly guide the skin back to the starting place. Then slide lightly an inch or so lower to begin again. When working on a small dog, hold the skin gently between the first section of our fingers and the pad of your thumb. Coiled Python TTouches on the legs help to calm, ground, and focus a dog.

## WHAT IT LOOKS LIKE

**1 Shoulders** It can be helpful in some cases to stabilize the dog between two hands. Here, I am showing the Coiled Python on the right shoulder. This position of connection combined with the TTouch makes the dog feel secure and balanced.

**2 Front Legs** When working on smaller dogs adjust the TTouch by using just two or three fingers. The thumb assists the fingers in the lifting motion.

**3-4 Hind Legs** I am combining an Abalone TTouch with a Python TTouch on the hind leg. My other hand is stabilizing the dog's leg lower down. I start on the top of the thigh and connect the TTouches down to the paw.

## Reduces sensitivity, increases confidence, stimulates circulation

# The Tarantulas Pulling the Plow TTouch

This TTouch is a variation on an ancient Mongolian method called "skin rolling." It releases fear, reduces touch sensitivity, and stimulates circulation. It is helpful for dogs that are nervous when touched, and dogs with limited body awareness. You can also increase your dog's trust in you. Try the Tarantulas Pulling the Plow TTouch on yourself, or on another person, to experience its relaxing effectiveness.

### HOW TO

Place your hands side by side on your dog's body. The tips of your fingers should "walk" forward in the direction of the movement

while your thumbs point to the side and lightly touch each other. Take a "step" of about one inch with both index fingers simultaneously, and allow the two thumbs to follow behind like a plow. The skin in front of your thumbs will be rolled gently. Next, take a step with the middle fingers. Your index fingers and middle fingers alternate, making steps while the thumbs are pulled along. All this should be done with an even, flowing motion. Run several of these "lines" from tail to head on different areas of your dog's back, parallel to his spine. "Walking off into the air" at the end of the line of Tarantulas has a nice carry-over effect your dog will enjoy.

To calm the dog, work slowly from his shoulders to his tail. To stimulate him, work more quickly and against the hair of his coat.

## WHAT IT LOOKS LIKE

**1–5 From the Back to the Head** Place your hands on either side of the spine. If he's concerned about having his hind end touched, start at the shoulders and gradually work your way back toward the tail. These pictures show the Tarantula TTouch from the back to the front, which is stimulating the dog's circulation.

## Relaxes, calms and stimulates

# Hair Slides

Doing Hair Slides is an excellent way of making a connection with your dog since it is relaxing for both of you. It provides a pleasant experience that is helpful for dogs afraid of being groomed. The root of the hair is connected to the nervous system, therefore it is an excellent TTouch for dogs with neurological problems.

## HOW TO

Take some between your thumb and index finger, or use the spaces between the fingers of your flat hand to gently slide up from the root of the hair to its end. You can also slide a lot of hairs through your fingers in one movement. Slide your open hand with slightly spread fingers into the coat, close the fingers, then gently glide your hand from the roots to the tips of the hair at a 90-degree angle.

Start as close as possible to the roots of the hair and follow the direction the hair grows. If you do the Hair Slides slowly and softly you will greatly add to your relationship with your dog. You will notice that these are not only relaxing for your dog, but you as well.

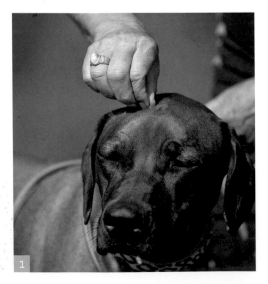

## WHAT IT LOOKS LIKE

**1 Head**  Most dogs like slow, gentle Hair Slides on their head. With this TTouch you can calm down a nervous or fearful dog and build a relationship. Hair Slides are also helpful for dogs that bark or whine constantly. Stabilize your dog's head by placing one hand under his muzzle.

**2 Shoulders**  Dogs that pull on the leash are hyperactive, nervous, or high-strung and usually very tense in the shoulders. Try these Hair Slides to relax them. Hair Slides done on a large area with the fingers of your flat hand lead to deep relaxation. Support the opposite shoulder with your other hand. On longhaired dogs, separate your fingers and glide upward through the hair.

**3–4  Back**  Hair Slides can be an enjoyable introduction to TTouch bodywork for dogs

### What should you do if...
#### ...the dog's hair is too short to do Hair Slides?

Lift your dog's skin up gently with your thumb and index finger, and slide along the hair while letting go of the skin very slowly. Be careful not to pinch your dog.

that do not readily accept other TTouches. Hair Slides on a dog's back create more awareness and flexibility in a gentle and loving way. You can work the large areas of the back with your whole hand, and smaller areas with your fingers.

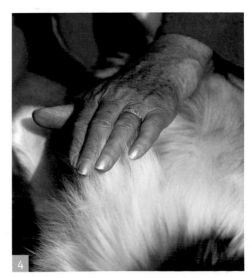

# The Lick of the Cow's Tongue

The Lick of the Cow's Tongue is one of the sliding TTouches. The light sliding motion across the hair from shoulder to the back and from midline to the spine improves the flexibility and fluidity of your dog's movement. This is excellent for dogs to enhance the weaving motions, jumps and turns in agility, and balance and flexibility in obedience classes. Use the Lick of the Cow's Tongue after a sports performance to return energy to the body. This TTouch increases circulation and improves the dog's body awareness.

## HOW TO

The Lick of the Cow's Tongue is relaxing when you use your flat hand, or stimulating when you use curved fingers. Start at the shoulder and slide your slightly spread and curved fingers to the top of the back, then from midline to the back. Start each slide a few inches apart until you reach the dog's hindquarters. To finish, you can softly stroke to the end of the the tail. This soothing TTouch improves the dog's well-being and balance.

## WHAT IT LOOKS LIKE

**1–4 Shoulders to Spine**  I start at the shoulder and lightly slide across the hair keeping my fingers lightly spread and curved. I continue along the dog's side up to the spine. I keep my fingers relaxed so they can smoothly glide through the dog's hair. Each slide is done just a few inches apart.

## What should you do if...
### ... your dog gets restless?

Make sure to keep your hands soft while they follow the contour of the dog's body, and breathe quietly and rhythmically. Use a flat hand and keep a "positive picture" in your mind.

# To end a session

# Noah's March

Noah's March is one of the sliding TTouches that we often use to end a TTouch session. The circular TTouches awaken awareness in different parts of the body while the smooth sliding strokes of Noah's March connect the entire body and integrate the circular TTouches.

## HOW TO

Place your hand lightly on the body and make a smooth sliding contact from the head, across the back and down the hindquarters. This can be done with the dog lying down as shown on p.65, or in a standing position. Most dogs prefer a light contact for this TTouch.

## WHAT IT LOOKS LIKE

**1 Shoulder**  Using a soft hand, I start at the shoulder and slide my hand along the back to the hip. The terrier is relaxed but still listening and enjoying the treatment.

**2–4 Body**  This position also works. I am mindfully sliding my hand along the dog's back to his hips. My fingers are slightly spread and I am making sure to keep a contact the terrier enjoys. This can also be done in a standing position.

You may be using too much pressure or holding your breath. If the dog is nervous about contact on the hindquarters, just cover the part that feels safe in the beginning. Be patient. Connect the part that is acceptable and over a few sessions extend the area when the dog trusts the contact.

# To get the dog's attention, calm or activate

# The Zigzag TTouch

The Zigzag TTouch is useful to make an initial contact or to get the attention of a nervous or hyperactive dog. When done slowly, it calms, and when done more briskly, it can stimulate or activate. The Zigzag TTouch connects the different parts of the body. It should be done rhythmically.

## HOW TO

The name of the Zigzag TTouch suggests the movement. With your fingers spread apart, move your hand across the hair in a line interspersed with five-degree changes of direction along the top of the back. Keep your wrist straight, and your fingers spread and relaxed. If you are working with a restless dog, make your slides a little faster for the first few Zigzags, then slow down.

## WHAT IT LOOKS LIKE

1–4 **Over the Top of the Body**  Start the Zigzag TTouch on the shoulder, With your fingers spread apart, move upward in a diagonal line to the spine. Then, with your fingers together, slide down the ribs in a diagonal line. Continue these sliding Zigzag movements to the hindquarters. When the dog is nervous use Zigzags on the same side of the body where you are standing or sitting rather than reaching over him.

The Zigzag TTouch is perfect for activating older or stiff dogs. Use several rows of Zigzag TTouches on both sides of the dog's body, starting at different spots so you can reach as many parts of the body as possible.

# The Inchworm

The Inchworm is done with both hands and works wonders by releasing tension in the shoulders, neck and back, particularly with fearful or nervous animals. The Inchworm was named after the way this worm moves along.

## HOW TO

Place both hands on the dog's back about two to four inches apart. Using just enough pressure to move the skin, gently push both hands together (toward each other), pause and release back into the position where you started. To enhance relaxation, make sure that your release takes about twice as long as it took to bring your hands together earlier. Repeat the Inchworm on different parts of the dog's back, and make sure to breathe deeply for even more relaxation: inhale as you are bringing your hands together, start the exhale during the pause, and end the exhale during the release.

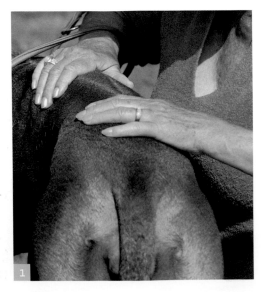

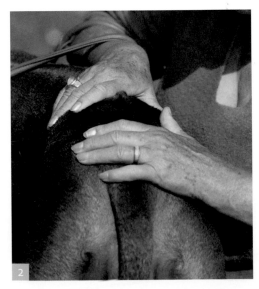

## WHAT IT LOOKS LIKE

**1–2** I am working on the back of a Rhodesian Ridgeback. Photo 1 shows the start position with my hands gently resting on the dog's back—not applying any downward pressure. I then slide my hands toward each other, moving the skin under my hands. Photo 2 shows how close my hands have come together—you can see some folds of the dog's skin between them.

**3–6** This terrier is relaxed—and loving the Inchworm along his back. I start at the neck and finish close to the tail to give the dog a new and pleasant feel of his frame. It is important not to let the weight of your hands and arms rest on the dog—there should be no downward pressure. Take some time with the Inchworm T Touch and it will become your dog's favorite.

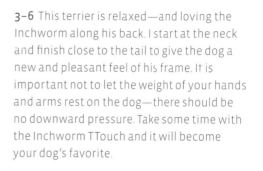

# Releases stress, tension and cramping

# The Belly Lift

Belly Lifts help dogs to relax their abdominal muscles, which aids with cramping and encourages deeper breathing. They are especially useful for dogs that are hyperactive, fearful, aggressive, nervous, pregnant, or ones that suffer from digestive upsets, arthritis in the legs, back problems and difficulty getting up. Caution! Do not use Belly Lifts when your dog has disc problems.

## HOW TO

You can perform the Belly Lift in various ways either with your hands, a towel, or an elastic bandage as these photos demonstrate. Whichever method you use, it's important to work slowly.

For example, you can gently support—pause—and lower the animal's abdomen with the same technique you used with the Python TTouch. Inhale or exhale as you lift, pause a moment, and slowly exhale as you return to your starting point. If you are using a bandage, continue the downward release until the bandage is loose and hanging below the dog's belly. The slow release is very important for getting the desired effect and will be your dog's favorite part. Start on the belly right behind the elbows and move toward the hindquarters with each additional Belly Lift. Keeping your body soft and comfortable while you do this will improve the quality of the Belly Lifts.

## WHAT IT LOOKS LIKE

**1–2 With Your Hand** Put your left hand under the abdomen and your right hand on the back of your dog. With your left hand apply pressure toward the spine, but only to the extent that your dog is comfortable. Hold this position then slowly release the contact. Remember that the slow release is the most important part.

**3–4 With an Elastic Bandage** I am demonstrating using a wrap. The Ridgeback's posture is showing that she is unsure. I start at the chest and take the bandage between her front legs so it sits in front of her shoulder on the right side, and behind the shoulder on her left side. Photo 4 shows that the dog is starting to relax—she is lowering her head and the tip of her tail is starting to relax.

## Case History
Shawnee, a Belgian Shepherd, about five years old, with weak hips.

Shawnee, my sister Robyn's dog, had weak hips and very straight back legs, which made it difficult for her to get up from the floor. X-rays showed that she had calcium deposits in the joints. In order to keep her pain at a minimum, Shawnee avoided having her weight on her hind legs, and as a result, she got tense in her back. Robyn helped her dog to relax these muscles by regularly performing lifts with a towel on Shawnee's hind legs. She pulled the towel between the hind legs, taking the weight off the dog's hips—just as in a Belly Lift. Robyn treated both sides and was able to relax the muscles and alleviate the pain. Of course, this TTouch does not replace veterinary treatment, but it is something you can do to help your dog and reduce pain.

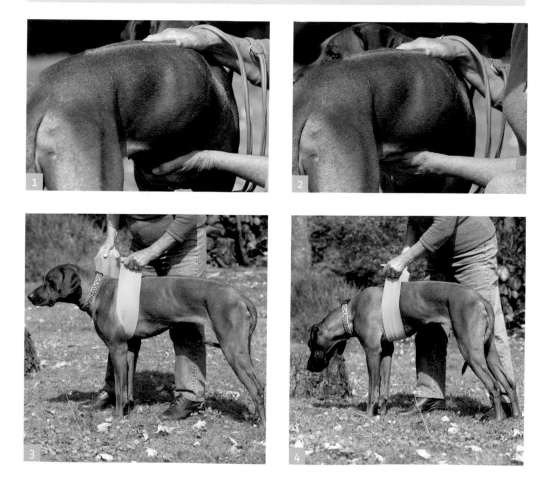

# The Mouth TTouch

TTouch on the mouth develops a sense of trust and focus and willingness to learn that is remarkable. This is such an valuable area to work on because of the connection to the limbic system—the part of the brain that controls emotions. It's wonderful for all dogs, but can change the attitude and behavior of dogs who are unfocused, inattentive, hyperactive, chronic barkers or resistant. It's great preparation for teeth cleaning, vet exams, and for show dogs who must accept mouth examination by a judge. It has been very effective for changing the behavior of aggressive dogs, but should be only used for aggressive dogs by experienced dog trainers or TTouch practitioners who work with aggressive animals.

## HOW TO

First begin with Lying Leopard TTouches on the neck and head and then move to the outside of the lips. When your dog rests his chin in your other hand, you can slide your finger under the lips and use gentle Raccoon TTouches on the gums. If a dog is restless or resistant, you may have to go back to the body and develop a trusting relationship working from shoulders to tail with a variety of TTouches, and then go back to the head. The Mouth TTouch takes patience and perseverance and perhaps several sessions to be successful but the outcome is worth the effort.

## WHAT IT LOOKS LIKE

**1–2 Lying Down**  Begin with soft Lying Leopard TTouches on the muzzle. When he is comfortable with this gently lift the lips and make light Raccoon TTouches on his gums. Keep your hands soft and be sure your dog is relaxed before proceeding.

**3–5 Sitting**  It's sometimes easier to begin with your dog in a sitting position. Notice how my left hand supports the chin while the other hand does Lying Leopard TTouches on the outside of the mouth. When that is acceptable do gentle Raccoon TTouches on top of the nose and lift the lips to TTouch the upper gums. Be patient and go step by step according to what your dog will accept. You can also extend your open hand under the dog's chin with the arm lightly stabilizing the dog's neck while you lift the lips gently with the fingers of your other hand.

## What should you do if...
### ... your dog is nervous about having his mouth touched?

If your dog is restless as you start the Mouth TTouch, check his teeth and gums. When a dog has plaque (brown stains on his teeth) or red inflamed gums, take him to your vet. If the gums and teeth seem healthy, check to see if his mouth is dry. When it is, wet your fingers with some water and try again. The Mouth TTouch gives you a good opportunity to regularly check your dog's mouth and gums.

Calms, focuses, reduces pain, prevents shock

# The Ear TTouch

The Ear TTouch is one of the most effective TTouches for calming excited or hyperactive dogs, as well as for activating dogs too calm or lethargic, or tired after competition or work. It has been used in thousands of cases for preventing shock or reducing shock after injury. The Ear TTouch can be of great assistance with all types of digestive disorders—nausea, constipation or diarrhea—always in conjunction with veterinary care. Ear TTouch activates the limbic system, effecting the emotions. It also influences all the important physical functions, appears to balance the immune system, and supports the body's ability to heal itself.

## HOW TO

Stabilize the dog's head with one hand. The thumb and the fingers of your other hand hold the opposite ear in such a way so that your thumb is on top. Change hands when you want to stroke the other ear. Gently stroke the ear with your thumb from the center of the head to the base of the ear and all the way to the tip. Work different areas with each slide so that you cover every square inch of the ear. With a floppy-eared dog, lift the ears gently so they are horizontal to the ground. Work upright ears in an upward direction.

Research on the effects of acupuncture has shown that stroking the ear affects the entire body: the Triple Heater Meridian runs along the bottom of the ear and it influences respiration, digestion and reproduction.

## WHAT IT LOOKS LIKE

**1–3 Slides** To relax your floppy-eared dog, begin with a slide from the center of the head, over the base of the ear to the tip, with a sideways move. Do this very gently between thumb and fingers. Support the head with your other hand.

**4–5 Circular TTouches** You can also use your thumb to make circular TTouches on the ear. Hold the ear parallel to the ground and work your circles around the edge of the ear until you come to the tip. Then, cover the entire ear with TTouches in parallel lines.

### What should you do if...
...the dog has heavy, floppy ears?

For heavy, floppy ears make your Ear Slides sideways so you don't pull down on the base of the ear as it can cause discomfort and even be painful.

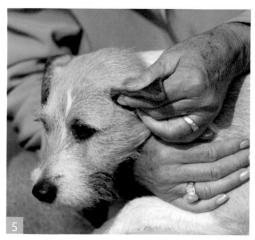

# Leg Circles with the Front Legs

Circling the front legs enhances a dog's mental, physical and emotional balance. The movement releases tense muscles in the neck and shoulders, and gives the dog a more secure connection to the ground. It's useful for improvement of gait and stride for competitive or working dogs, as well as for dogs who are shy; reactive to loud noises, other dogs, or strangers; insecure in new surroundings; or cautious about walking on slippery surfaces.

### HOW TO

You can circle the front legs with your dog standing, sitting, or lying down.

Do not force the movement. You want to be able to pick up the leg without resistance. If it's difficult, change the position. Begin in whichever position is the easiest. The idea is to improve balance by releasing tension without stretching the leg. Explore the range of motion in small circles. If the dog tries to pull the leg away, fold the paw back against the leg or gently move it in the direction the dog is pulling.

You may find that you can move one leg more easily than the other. Such a difference can be the result of tension, lack of balance, or an old injury, which you can improve with other TTouches on the leg or shoulder.

## WHAT IT LOOKS LIKE

**1–2 Standing** Support the dog with one hand on the elbow and the other holding lightly below the stifle joint. Move the leg forward with support at the elbow and backward with your hand softly guiding the shoulder. For the circles toward the ground, hold the paw in your hand and support the shoulder in the beginning to keep the dog balanced. Avoid pushing or stretching the leg to achieve maximum movement.

**3 Sitting** You can apply the same movement when the dog is sitting. I am supporting the opposite shoulder with my left hand.

**4 Lying Down** The Leg Circles can also be

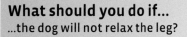

### What should you do if...
#### ...the dog will not relax the leg?

A dog may be resistant to the circles at first if he is sensitive about his feet being touched or nails trimmed. Begin with the Python TTouches from the elbow to the paw, and do Raccoon TTouches on the pads. Support the body with your other hand on the elbow or shoulder as shown here in the drawing and photos. Be patient, pay attention to your breathing and your own posture to be sure your own position is comfortable.

done with a relaxed dog lying on his side. Support the shoulder with your other hand.

Improves balance and coordination

# Leg Circles with the Hind Legs

With these Hind Leg Circles you can increase a dog's confidence. Range of motion and freedom of movement teach him new ways of using his body. Working and sporting dogs gain more awareness of their body and learn to use it more efficiently. Hind Leg Circles also relax the muscles all the way to the back, which help to calm tense or nervous dogs and those afraid of loud noises. Do not use Hind Leg Circles on older dogs or those with arthritis or hip dysplasia.

## HOW TO

These circles can be done standing or lying down. Standing is most useful for enhancing balance, and lying down is useful for increasing range of motion. When working with small or medium-size dogs, it is easier to have them on a table. In a standing position, support the hind leg of a large dog with one hand on the stifle and the lifting hand below the hock. If the dog is well-balanced, your supporting hand can be on the chest. Make small circles at the height that is easiest for a dog to balance and make movements in both directions only as far back or forward as it is easy.

## WHAT IT LOOKS LIKE

**1–4 Lying Down**  The whole leg from the hip to the paw is moved in gentle circles with one hand lifting the stifle and the other over the hock. When the leg relaxes, your hand slides below the hock to support the paw. The dog should stay as relaxed as this terrier is when the leg extends backward. In Photo 4, the stifle is being rotated in both directions.

**5 Standing**  Draw the circles small enough so it is easy for the dog to balance and you feel no resistance. Make sure the circles are round and the movement fluid. With a small dog, one hand on the chest can help maintain balance. With a larger dog, it may be more effective to give support under the chest.

## What should you do if...
### ... the dog limps or favors a leg?

Careful Leg Circles with very small movements, in a lying position, can help to
rehabilitate a limb after surgery. Even
after an injury has healed the memory of
the pain can remain so that protecting
the leg becomes habitual. Gentle circles,
first on the more stable leg, can bring a
sense of confidence and restore the use
of the leg.

# TTouches on the Paws

These TTouches are useful for dogs who are:

- Fearful, aggressive, not grounded, hyperactive
- Sensitive to noise—thunder, in particular
- Uneasy about their paws being touched
- Resistant to nail clipping
- Fearful about walking on an "unusual" surface, such as a slippery floor

## HOW TO

Your dog can sit, lie down, or stand. Do some of the TTouches your dog finds most relaxing. Starting at the top of the leg, do Clouded Leopard TTouches all the way down to the paws. If your dog is concerned about having his legs or feet touched, change the TTouch you are using or go back to where you had his trust and confidence. A short break can be useful when your dog is particularly resistant. Do gentle Lying Leopard TTouches on a paw, covering the whole area, and if your dog is ticklish between the pads, work with less pressure on these areas by using the Orangutan TTouch (p. 53). If he has long hair between the pads, he can be extra ticklish, so trim the hair first before attempting to trim his nails (see Toenail Trimming, p. 83).

## WHAT IT LOOKS LIKE

**1–4 Leg to Paw**  Start on the leg with connected TTouches until you reach the paw.

**5–6 On the Paw**  This Jack Russell is relaxed on his side while I am using connected Clouded Leopard Touches on his paws. When your dog will stay this comfortable while having his paw TTouched, toenail clipping becomes a breeze!

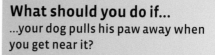

### What should you do if...
...your dog pulls his paw away when you get near it?

Use a piece of sheepskin and travel down the leg with the soft material using connected TTouches; you can also use a feather or paintbrush to add different textures. The next step is to touch the dog's paw with his other paw (p. 82). You can also offer your dog some treats to make the experience more pleasant.

# TTouches with the Paws

The idea of TTouching a dog with his own paw seems strange at first sight, especially since the area of the body that can be reached with a paw is not very large. But the goal of this exercise is to reduce the sensitivity of the paws and make your dog feel safe so that it will be easier for you to work on them regularly. Try it and you may be surprised by the result.

## HOW TO

**TTouch on the Leg**  I am putting the dog's left paw on her right leg and making a few circles with the paw on the leg. It is important for the dog to keep her leg relaxed and free in order to protect her joints. I guide the TTouching paw down the leg as long as it is comfortable for her, and she is relaxed and paying attention.

# A stress-free procedure

# Toenail Trimming

It is important to trim a dog's nails regularly if he does not wear them down in daily life. Toenails that are too long can badly affect a dog's posture: instead of putting his weight on the entire paw he will shift it to the back of the pad. This unnatural position can lead to soreness and tension throughout his body.

## HOW TO

With some exceptions, the nails should be short enough so that you do not hear them click on a hard floor. However, be careful not to cut the nails too short. With a difficult dog you may need another person's help. Only cut a few nails at a time, and give your dog several breaks. Many dogs are less resistant to an electric drill than to the nail clippers, and feel more comfortable in a standing position with the paw on the front leg folded back. Let your dog choose if he is more comfortable standing, sitting or lying down.

## WHAT IT LOOKS LIKE

**1 TTouch with Clippers**  To get the dog used to clippers and to trust you, use the tool to make circular TTouches on the dog's leg.

**2 Cutting**  It is important that you are careful when cutting nails; be sure that your non-clipping hand is not squeezing the paw too hard while you are using the clippers.

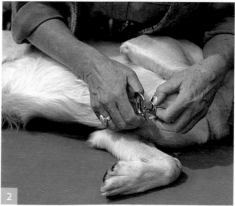

# The Tail TTouch

With Tail Work and the Tail TTouches, you can help your dog overcome fear and timidity (including fear of loud noises, such as thunder and fireworks). This work can also be helpful with dogs that react around other dogs. And, in addition to vet care, the Tail TTouch may ease pain and promote recovery after injury or surgery.

## HOW TO

The way a dog carries his tail has many different meanings. If he is wagging his tail in a relaxed manner, he is calm. A nervous, hyperactive, or insecure dog may wag his tail constantly and very fast. When a dog holds his tail in a stiff, still, and high position, he is indicating dominance or aggression, while a dog who carries his tail between his legs is demonstrating fear and submission. Whatever the position of the tail, you can influence your dog's behavior by changing the way he carries it.

Start with Lying Leopard TTouches around the base of the tail; follow them with Raccoon TTouches or Hair Slides along the entire tail to relax the dog and build trust. When your dog's tail is tight do some TTouches with it on the inside of his leg, or run the back of your hand under his tail to avoid him having the feeling of being grabbed.

Circling the tail helps to release tension at its base. Hold the tail close to the base with a soft and slightly open hand to avoid squeezing. Your other hand supports the body where it is comfortable (under the belly or on the chest). Gently guide the tail in small circles going in both directions.

Holding the tail at the base, gently and slowly stretch it, then pause and release it even more slowly. You can also gently slide your hand down the tail as you release it. Monitor your breathing, inhale as you stretch, and exhale on the release.

## WHAT IT LOOKS LIKE

**1 Before** Nina is insecure so she is tucking her tail between her legs. I start with the Troika TTouch on her thigh and croup to gain her trust.

**2–4 Changing the Tail Carriage** I am using my right hand to stabilize the dog and my left hand to free her tail from its clamped position. I am lifting it carefully to change the dog's posture, then I slide my hand further down the tail and gently move it up and down. Later, I'll move it in circles in both directions.

**5 Stretching the Tail** I take a light traction on the tail, hold and slowly release to relax the spine and give the dog a new sense of her body. Nina's tail is now relaxed and swings freely when she moves.

# Tellington TTouch Training Equipment

We use special equipment to help dogs find their balance—not just physical balance, but mental and emotional. In the dog world there is new equipment being developed every year and we are constantly searching for the best solutions for dogs and their owners. You will find descriptions and suggestions for their use in the following pages.

## Why Do We Use This Equipment?

To teach a dog to walk on a leash without pulling is a matter of balance for dogs and their owner. Many behavioral as well as physical issues develop from leash-pulling, and many shelter dogs don't get adopted because of this behavior.

The Tellington Method for teaching a dog to walk in balance without pulling on the leash is very effective. With the special leash combinations it takes surprisingly little time to teach a dog to walk in balance without the use of force or dominance.

### Bring Your Dog into Balance

Leash pulling is a common problem that many dog owners ignore because they don't know what to do about it and do not realize the physical damage it can cause from pressure on the vertebrae of the neck and back as well as the pasterns, shoulders, hips and knees.

We have multiple tools to bring dogs into balance so they stop pulling:
- Head halter (Holt, Gentle Leader, Black Dog, Snoot Loop, and others)
- Harness (Step-In, H-Harness, Easy Walker, and others)
- "Suitcase" Harness
- Balance Leash
- Balance Leash Plus
- Super-Balance Leash

*Working dogs through the various obstacles of the Playground for Higher Learning takes them beyond instinctive behavior so they become more adaptable in new situations. Hyperactive dogs become grounded; shy or fearful dogs develop confidence; reactive dogs learn self-control and to think rather than react; and a cooperative attitude and bonding results between people and their dog.*

*A dog this strong and pulling with all his weight against the leash puts extreme pressure on the neck vertebrae, as well as stress on the front and hind leg joints. And his breathing will be compromised, too.*

*This is the Balance Leash Plus, which quickly allows you to bring your dog back into balance and stop the pulling.*

*The Harness helps to keep a dog straight—and stops spinning, rearing or backing away.*

When there is constant pressure on the leash, the dog pulls even more. And, this can cause injury to the person on the other end of the leash. When a small dogs pulls, it is often ignored because he is not strong enough to bother most people, but there is just as much stress on his body as there is on the largest dog.

To help your dog find his balance use a Balance Leash, a Balance Leash Plus, or the harness—keeping the leash in both hands.

The Tellington equipment consists of a number of different options for changing unwanted behavior, such as using a head halter combined with a flat regular collar or harness, the Body Wrap, Thundershirt, T-Shirt and many more that will be explained in detail on the following pages. We also use a Wand, a stiff horse whip unusual in traditional dog training (see top photo, p. 5). You can calm down a nervous dog by touching him all over with the Wand. Stroking the dog's legs calms and focuses him.

We adapted use of the Wand from our

experiences with horses—it is a very useful tool in many situations. As mentioned in the previous chapter, a dog that won't accept being touched by your hand when you are handling him is often much more compliant when stroked with the Wand instead. Leading the dog is easier, too, when you use the wand as an extension of your arm to show the way.

## The Equipment

The following is a list of the special Tellington TTouch Training equipment:

- **Flat Collar:** This is the basic Tellington TTouch tool for every dog and can be used in combination with a head halter. We use the flat collar in place of a choke chain, slip collar, or pinch (prong) collar.
- **Harness:** A chest harness for dogs (p. 96).
- **Head Halter:** We use a variety of head halters, such as the Holt or Snoot Loop (p. 98).
- **Holt** (formerly called a Halti): A special head halter for dogs that allows the handler to control the dog's head more easily than a collar.
- **Snoot Loop:** Very similar to the Holt, but more appropriate for dogs with a short muzzle.
- **Leash with Two Snaps:** This leash should be about six to eight feet long with two snaps, one stronger, and one lighter (see illustration, p. 96). If you have difficulty finding a double-snap leash, you can order one from the Tellington TTouch office, see www.ttouch.com.
- **Body Wrap:** This consists of one or two elastic bandages, two or three inches wide. Bandages are available in all sizes, choose one suitable for your dog (p. 102).

- **The Wand:** A three-foot long, stiff horse-whip. To make sure the Wand does not get caught in the dog's hair, it should have a smooth surface (see photo, p. 5).

## Safety First

- A Golden Rule: Keep the exercises short so that your dog has enough time to process what he has learned and not be stressed by too much input.
- Proceed one step at a time; raise your expectations gradually; and give the dog plenty of breaks.
- When using the Playground for Higher Learning, remember to ask the dog to walk slowly. Learning is enhanced in the slower gaits.
- The more versatility you can teach, the more adaptable and mentally flexible the dog will become. Change direction with each obstacle and lead your dog from both sides.
- Be generous with your praise, use TTouches, a happy voice and sometimes, food treats.
- Learn the dog's body language and "calming signals." Watch his posture and expression to see how he is feeling.
- Be very careful when working with unfamiliar, fearful or aggressive dogs. Don't put too much pressure on these dogs; they may respond by growling or biting. If you are not a trained professional, do not work with an aggressive dog.
- Do not stare at a nervous or aggressive dog in the eyes. Many dogs experience this as a threat. If you are greeting a dog or want to put on a Holt or Body Wrap, it is safest to approach the dog from the side.

This dog is wearing a Holt. The nosepiece needs to be loose enough so that the dog can open his mouth to pant, pick up a toy or take a treat.

Leash pulling is often ignored in small dogs, but it is important to remember that damage can be done to them when they are allowed to pull. The two points of contact on this harness inhibit pulling and a harness is more comfortable for most than a collar.

The Body Wrap gives a feeling of containment and support. It calms dogs who are unfocused, hyperactive or afraid of loud noises, gives confidence to shy dogs; and gives a sense of stability to older dogs.

# The Balance Leash

To put on the Balance Leash rearrange your regular leash in a position across the dog's lower chest. Walk even with the dog's head and your body turned slightly toward the dog, and hold the leash in both hands between your thumb and index finger. If you dog pulls, use an upward signal to shift your dog's center of gravity back and release the contact. When this happens, he can find his own balance on all four feet and is better able to respond to your signals.

## HOW TO

The leash should be at least six feet long. Attach the leash to the dog's collar as usual, and drape it around your dog's chest. Hold the loop of the leash with one hand and the end of the leash with the other (see drawing). Using both hands for two points of contact is the secret to success. To slow down or stop, rebalance your dog with two or three subtle, light "ask-and-release" movements of your fingers on the leash. You want to stop your dog from leaning and to shift his weight over all four feet. A second secret to success is to make sure that the end of the leash that is attached to the collar remains loose. Check the snap that is attached to the collar. This should be loose and lie flat.

With small dogs it is sometimes difficult to keep the leash on the chest because they have a tendency to step over the loop, twist or back out. In these cases we recommend using a harness or a head halter when they pull. With larger breeds of dogs these can be very effective—except for dogs who spin, lunge, rear or back up. In these cases we recommend the Balance Leash Plus, Super-Balance Leash, or a harness with two points of contact or a ring on the chest to attach the leash.

# The Balance Leash Plus

If you only have a flat collar and regular leash and the dog suddenly starts to pull because he sees a cat or another dog, you can turn your regular collar and harness into the Balance Leash Plus in an instant. It allows you to keep your dog from pulling and brings both you and the dog back into balance.

## HOW TO

On your dog's right side, stand even with the collar and slide your left hand down toward the snap attached to the flat collar. Hold the end of the leash with your right hand and drop the slack onto the ground right behind your dog's left elbow. Ask your dog to step through the slack with his left front foot only and raise the leash to contact the dog's sternum. Take the end of the leash and thread it underneath the collar coming up from the bottom (see photo).

When the dog pulls be sure that the end of the leash attached to the collar stays loose and that you catch his forward movement with the part of the leash that is across his chest. It is also important to immediately release the pressure when his weight is over his feet. It may be necessary to rebalance him several times to help him be able to maintain this balance. Talk to your dog rather than give him an obedience command: you want him to develop his own self-control, not just follow commands. With a bit of practice, you'll be able to handle the leash with just one hand.

**Note:** Keep your hands over the top of the dog's back—don't pull him forward or backward. The Balance Leash and the Balance Leash Plus are just temporary tools used for training, not what you should use when going for a long walk. For walks, switch to a well-fitting harness in combination with a head halter or flat collar, or a Super-Balance Leash.

## Leading with the harness

# The Super-Balance Leash

During the past few years we have noticed that the Balance Leash when combined with the Step-In Harness works very well for many dogs. This leading technique improves balance and coordination and allows you to lead the dog with one hand, or if the situation requires, to quickly switch into leading with two hands. A leash with two snaps, one on either end, works best.

### HOW TO

This stuffed toy is a great model for the Super-Balance Leash—which is the striped rope in the photo. Attach its first snap to the ring on the harness above the dog's shoulders. Thread the smaller snap through the loop or ring in front of the chest and attach to the ring on the dog's opposite shoulder. The secret to success is for you to always stay even with the dog's neck when leading: if you walk behind the dog's shoulder, he will have a tendency to pull more. If your dog twists and circles a lot, try the "Suitcase" Harness (p. 95).

# The "Suitcase" Harness

The Suitcase helps the dog with a tendency to spin or jump up while you are trying to lead him. It enables you to keep him straight and shift his balance back onto all four feet. In addition to your regular leash, you will need another one, or a rope with two snaps, which is attached to the Step-In Harness. Note: The Suitcase is not suitable for a dog who is timid or sensitive to contact on his body.

## HOW TO

This toy dog is wearing the Super-Balance Leash—the striped rope in the photo. This can also be a double-clip leash. The "Suitcase," as explained below, is the blue rope in my left hand. Place the middle of this rope on your dog's back with both snaps hanging down. Cross the snaps under the dog's belly and attach them to the shoulder rings on opposite sides. Make sure that the opening of the snap points outward and away from the dog.

Now take the middle of this rope sitting on your dog's back and pull it up high enough so you can make a knot to create an approximate ten-inch loop (as shown), depending on the size of your dog and the length of your rope. Take the loop forward and place it between the two harness rings of a Step-In Harness above the shoulders. Now, take the snap of the Super-Balance Leash and attach it to the ring on the Harness above the dog's shoulders.

# Harnesses

Since we started using TTouch with dogs in the early 90's the choice and variety of harnesses has grown enormously. There used to be only a few and most had the leash attachment so far back on the dog's back that it was easy for the dog to pull. Now, however, many dog lovers have successfully corrected leash-pulling by using the newer harnesses available. Other people, even those whose dogs don't usually pull, prefer to use a harness because it takes pressure off the dog's neck.

## HOW TO

It is in your interest to bring a dog into balance because there is a link between physical, mental and emotional balance. Some harnesses on the market, especially those with the ring on the chest, work by pulling the dog off balance. While this may make it harder for the dog to pull, it can also encourage him to react badly or make him fearful.

There are a number of good harnesses available like the Step-In, the H-Harness and the Control-Ease Harness. A harness can be

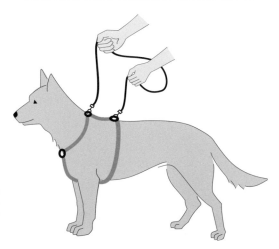

used in combination with a head halter or flat collar so you have two points of influence to help balance a dog. The harnesses described here come in a large variety of colors and size. Some dogs will be fine with the leash attached on one ring; however, we find that many dogs benefit from a double-snapped leash attached at two points of contact. This might be at two separate rings on the harness, or attached to the harness and the collar or head halter. This increases your ability to influence the dog and give clear signals. It is possible to hold the loop of the leash in one hand, or for greater influence, with two hands. This configuration with two points of contact is especially useful with a dog that pulls, is unfocused, fearful, or reactive.

Many harnesses have improved their fit to make the dog comfortable. Every one has it pros and cons: look for a harness that allows enough room for the dog's shoulders, and with the ring on top of the dog's back not set too far to the rear.

## WHAT IT LOOKS LIKE

**1 Step-In**  Here, Durga, the stuffed dog is showing the combination of the Step-In Harness and a head halter.

**2 Control Ease Harness**  This harness is sold with a leash that clips to the ring on the front of the chest, and also at the shoulders.

**3 H-Type Harness**  The H-Harness has a leash ring close enough to the shoulder to encourage the dog to be in balance. When the leash is clipped further back, the dog is encouraged to pull.

**4. H-Type Harness from Above**  This is an example of the two points of contact on this harness and using a double-ended leash.

# Introducing the Head Halter

If your dog is young, hyperactive, unfocused, disobedient, aggressive toward other dogs, or pulls on the leash, you might choose a head halter (Holt or Snoot Loop) for the Leading Exercises. We use it in combination with a flat collar. The advantage of using a Holt is that you can control your dog with a lot less force than just using a normal collar, and you can easily turn your dog's head to direct his attention. It is important to buy a head halter that fits the dog well.

## HOW TO

A head halter combined with a flat collar or harness is a useful tool for many dogs. The advantage of a head halter is that you are able to guide your dog more effectively and with more precision. You are able to turn your dog's head away when he wants to chase a bicycle, a running child, or is involved in an argument with another dog. You can easily bring his attention back to you. If you have a very energetic or strong dog, he should always wear a head halter.

## WHAT IT LOOKS LIKE

1 To prepare the dog for the Holt, Robyn places the leash over Shawnee's nose. If the dog wants to push the leash off, let him do it and quietly put it back on. With some dogs this can take a bit of time so support him with some TTouches and short practice sessions.

2 Next, to prepare Shawnee for the contact and confinement of the Holt, Robyn TTouches around the mouth and covers the dog's muzzle with her hands. She then takes some sewing elastic and loosely places it around Shawnee's muzzle while talking to her in a soft voice.

3 Now Robyn crosses the elastic under Shawnee's muzzle, takes both ends to the back of the neck, and makes a knot that is easy to undo. The elastic is loose enough so the dog can easily pant or accept a treat. To get the dog really comfortable with the elastic, feed some treats, apply some TTouches, and play a little or take her through the Playground for Higher Learning. This creates enough distraction to get the dog to accept the unfamiliar feeling on her head.

4 Shawnee is ready for the Holt and Robyn shows it to her. Make sure you are practiced (use a toy to learn on) in order to avoid a lot of confusion and fumbling when you put it on the dog for the first time. A treat can be

helpful to get your dog to love putting his nose into the Holt.

**5** Robyn places the Holt over the elastic and closes the snap at the dog's neck. She combines the elastic with the Holt in order to get Shawnee to accept the Holt quickly and easily. Your dog should wear the Holt for a while without a leash attached to it.

**6** The leash should be light and about six to eight feet long. Attach one end to the flat collar, and the other one to the bottom ring of the Holt. Hold the leash in both hands.

# Leading with the Head Halter

The goal to successfully leading the dog with a head halter is a dog who responds to the lightest signals and, later on, one who can be lead in a flat collar or harness on a loose leash.

Leading a dog with a Holt may be a somewhat unusual experience in the beginning. We recommend you hold the leash, which is attached to the Holt and the collar, with both hands. After you have practiced it for some time, you will notice how simple and comfortable it is—and how much easier it is to control your dog.

## HOW TO

Holt Training is a very helpful way of teaching your dog to respond to very light signals and not to pull. When you are leading your dog with both hands you should be very conscious of which part of the leash you use first. For example, when you want to start walking, give your first signal on the collar, and when you want to turn your dog, give the first signal on the Holt. Many people habitually hold the leash tight clenching their fist—even when their dog is not

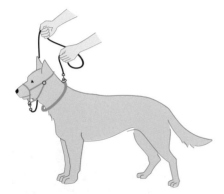

moving at all. Practice keeping a slack leash at all times when your dog is not moving. He should stand in self-balance and not lean on the leash because pulling always leads to more pulling. You can change your dog's habit of pulling on the leash by changing your own leading habits as well.

## WHAT IT LOOKS LIKE

**1 Neutral Position**  This is the "neutral" position: If you are standing on the right side of your dog your right hand holds the end of the leash that is attached to the Holt, while your left hand holds the end that is attached to the collar. Both parts of the leash should have a little slack. Position yourself next to your dog's head. To ensure that your contact is light enough, place your thumbs forward along the leash.

**2 Start Walking**  To ask your dog to start walking, gently tug at the part of the leash attached to the collar and release it immediately. Do not expect your dog to start walking when you tug—the release is the signal to move. Your verbal signals are important as well. Combine your movement on the leash with a "Let's go!" If your dog is excitable, choose a softer communication like "This way," spoken while you move your body forward.

**3 Turning** If you want to turn your dog in your direction gently signal with the part of the leash that is attached to the Holt. You should announce all turns with a quiet signal on the Holt, and follow it with a signal on the collar. Alternate your signals to guide your dog through the turn.

**4 Turning Away from You** If you want to turn your dog away from you, point your feet where you want to go and turn your body in that direction as well. Give the dog a verbal cue and place the end of the leash attached to the Holt against the dog's muzzle to indicate the direction you want him to turn Slow him down with the collar and walk toward his shoulder. This encourages the dog to turn away from you, and your body position helps him make a smooth turn.

# The Body Wrap

The Body Wrap enhances your dog's sense of his own body and makes him more confident in his movement and behavior. It is especially beneficial for dogs afraid of loud noises, ones that are nervous and hyperactive or that panic when riding in a car. The Body Wrap also helps injured dogs to recover, and it is helpful for older, stiff, and arthritic dogs. There are several versions of wrapping. Experiment to find out the type of Body Wrap most appropriate for your dog.

## HOW TO

You can use elastic bandages (wraps) from the drug store (Ace bandages work best). Make sure that the bandage lies flat on the dog and that long-haired dogs don't have their coat ruffled or sticking up. When the wrap is too loose it loses its effect; however, you don't want it so tight that it restricts movement. To help dogs frightened of thunder and other loud noise, make sure the wrap is snug enough to give comfort, but not tight. If your dog seems uncomfortable, take the Body Wrap off.

## WHAT IT LOOKS LIKE

1 Elastic Bandages   Different colored bandages can have a different effect on the dog: red activates, blue calms, and green stimulates. Ace bandages can by dyed many colors.

2 Baby Diaper Pins   These pins are the safest to use—available at most drugstores

3 Head Wrap   The Head Wrap is good preparation for wearing a head halter or preparing the dog for TTouches on the head.

4–5 Half Wrap   The Half Wrap is used mainly on dogs nervous about having their

hindquarters wrapped, or on dogs that have knee or hip problems. Place the center of the bandage across the dog's chest, then cross the ends on the back and under the belly. Take both ends up to the back and secure them with a safety pin. You can pull the back part of the wrap forward when working with male dogs.

## 6 Half Wrap—A Second Version

This variation of the Half Wrap starts on top of the neck with one-third of the bandage on the left side and two-thirds on the right side. Bring both ends forward, come between the front legs and take the longer end once around the belly. Attach the ends of the bandage by using a safety pin.

## For security and confidence

# The **T-Shirt**

If your dog is **fearful**, shy, reactive or overly excited and makes your life difficult, the T-Shirt can be the answer to your problems. It is also useful for dogs that are sensitive to sounds, have separation **anxiety**, or are restless in the car. It can help with uncontrollable barking and leash-pulling because the T-Shirt gives the dog a "frame" through which he can better feel his body. There are quite a few different shirts on the market: check out your local pet store or the Internet.

## HOW TO

When you dress your dog in the shirt, stand or crouch beside him and have a treat ready. Make sure he does not feel crowded while you dress him—it's a good idea to practice on a toy dog so you have the movement down. Do not let him wear the T-Shirt unsupervised. If you use a human T-Shirt, put it on with the chest of the shirt on the dog's back.

## WHAT IT LOOKS LIKE

**1–2 T-Shirt**  Using a child's T-Shirt is the easiest option. Depending on your dog's size you may need to tighten the shirt around the belly with a rubber band or hair tie.

**3–4 Fleece Shirt**  When it is cold you may substitute a T-Shirt for a Fleece Shirt to keep your dog warm and comfortable.

**5–6 Thundershirt**  The Thundershirt is made of 98 percent cotton and 2 percent stretch material. It is easy to fit, sits snugly on the dog, and with the help of Velcro, is

## Case History
**Roy, the Belgian Shepherd.**

My sister, Robyn Hood, had a lot of success when she used a Thundershirt on her Belgian Shepherd, Roy. Roy refused to go up or down the stairs after they had been recarpeted. He was scared of the different texture and color. Robyn says, "When we changed the carpet on the stairs, he was extremely hesitant about going up and down. So I just put on a Thundershirt with a figure-eight wrap over the top of it to connect him to his hindquarters, did a little Far Work, and he was able to overcome his concern. I had to repeat this on a couple of other occasions, for example, when we changed the flooring in the office, but each time he regained his confidence and was able to walk on these new surfaces."

easy to put on. You can order a Thundershirt in green with the TTouch logo from www.ttouch.com. Thundershirts carry a money-back guarantee.

# The Journey of the Homing Pigeon

Being led by two people improves a dog's ability to learn: both sides of his brain are activated and he receives information and a sense of security from both sides of his body.

The Journey of the Homing Pigeon is a technique for leading animals from both sides. I have been using it for many years to guide and control difficult horses. This method is just as effective with dogs. Nervous animals gain confidence because they are given a clear direction, and are not able to charge ahead. In addition, some dogs feel protected by having people on both sides of them. This leading position is particularly effective for working with overactive, unfocused dogs.

## HOW TO

When you lead a dog from both sides you need two leashes, a flat collar, a harness, and sometimes, a Wand. Attach both leashes to the collar and one of them to the harness. There should be a space between the attachments of the two leashes on the collar so that you do not give signals on the same spot: this is confusing to the dog. The two people should walk at the head of the dog at a distance of about three feet out to the side. They should coordinate their signals: the signals for start, stop, and turn should be given clearly.

To achieve smooth cooperation it is best if one person acts as the primary leader giving the signal, with the other person reinforcing it. It's a good idea, in most instances, for the dog's owner to be one of the people leading; two strangers should lead only when the dog is comfortable with them. Dogs that are aggressive toward other dogs can be con-trolled very safely in the Homing Pigeon. However, we do not recommend working with dogs that are aggressive toward people. Leave that to an experienced dog trainer who uses positive reinforcement, or call one of our dog practitioners who specialize in aggressive dogs.

## WHAT IT LOOKS LIKE

1 Slalom  Chablis is showing the Slalom, challenging his handlers to use precise body language and finely tuned, leash-handling skills. It is difficult to always stay even with the dog's shoulder—and stay out of his way—as he performs his turns. When the dog hesitates it can be helpful if the person who is less familiar to him gives him more space. The cones should be about one-dog-length apart so the exercise is not too difficult.

**2–3 Cavalletti**  Lisa and I are leading Giacomo over the Cavalletti. The poodle is wearing a flat collar and a harness, with the leashes attached to the harness. I am the leader, Lisa the support person. Stopping in the middle of the obstacle strengthens his trust and confidence.

**4 Ladder**  Karin and Gabi are leading Chablis over the Ladder. She is Karin's dog, so Karin is the leader. The dog is nicely straight and balanced as she steps through the obstacle. Note that Karin and Gabi are even with the dog's shoulder and have loose leashes.

**5 Wire Mesh and Plastic Surfaces**  We placed a lot of different surfaces one after another. Sylvia and I show this new obstacle to Giacomo. I'm handling the leash with one hand and using the Wand on the ground to encourage the dog to look where he is going.

# The Playground for Higher Learning®

Dogs enjoy working in the Playground for Higher Learning. You have probably watched dogs enthusiastically competing on an agility course, flying over jumps, rushing through a tunnel, and having a great time. In the Tellington Method, we work with obstacles, not for agility competition, but to develop awareness and confidence. We find we can develop a dog's willingness to focus and listen, to wait for our signals, and to overcome aggression or timidity. Your dog learns how to think and cooperate, because he has to concentrate on a given task.

## Why Do We Work with the Playground for Higher Learning?

Dogs become more intelligent and adapt easily to different circumstances when they can learn at their own speed and have fun while doing so. When dogs have the opportunity to learn new things in a relaxed atmosphere, their day-to-day life becomes easier.

Dogs enjoy working with obstacles and love to master small challenges. You may have already seen how enthusiastically dogs master the Slalom or how they concentrate as they walk through the Labyrinth, carefully listening to their handler and not stepping on the poles.

Having fun is not the only important aspect of the Playground for Higher Learning. It also enhances the dog's attention span, obedience and intelligence. He will learn to think and cooperate instead of just reacting instinctively. You will notice how quickly his ability to concentrate improves and how his body awareness changes. He will soon become more flexible and fluid in his movement.

### Praise

Letting your dog know when he has been successful is very important. Praise him for every small step in the right direction using a loving voice, TTouches or food. This will keep your dog happy and motivated. Switch your rewards frequently: sometimes a few nice words will do, or some TTouches will settle the dog, and let him know you are there for him.

When using food be careful. If you keep feeding constantly, the dog will not get a chance to think and learn and only thinks about the next treat coming his way.

Food helps to activate the parasympathetic nervous system, overriding the sympathetic nervous system which is activated in cases of fear or aggression (fight or flight). The parasympathetic nervous system is activated as soon as there is food in the mouth. This system is responsible for relaxation and necessary to support learning.

The Labyrinth is an especially important aspect of the Playground for Higher Learning and the effects of the Labyrinth have been studied extensively. Children with

*Walking on a narrow, low board teaches balance, body awareness, focus and gives a sense of confidence in new surroundings. It helps dogs ride quietly in a car or deal with crowds.*

learning disabilities have shown that walking through the Labyrinth improves their coordination and movement.

Likewise, work with dogs and horses in the Labyrinth has shown remarkable improvement in these animals' attention, coordination, and cooperation as well as physical, emotional and mental balance.

Leading the dog over different surfaces, such as wood or plastic, is excellent preparation for situations you may encounter when taking your dog to a place where he may have to cross a metal grid or walk on a slippery hardwood floor.

Poles on the ground, the Star, Cavalletti, the Board Walk and the Teeter Totter (Seesaw) teach the dog balance and coordination and are fun to master.

### The Obstacles

- For **the Labyrinth**, narrow boards or plastic PVC pipe work well. They should be eight to twelve feet long, and one to three inches wide. You can use shorter length boards (approximately three feet long) and assemble them or join them with connectors. These shorter pieces are easier to store. You can use the same boards or pipes for training the dog with the Poles, the Star, and the Cavalletti.
- **A board:** It should be about eight feet long, one foot wide, and one inch thick. With a round wooden block underneath, it can be turned into the Teeter-Totter (Seesaw). With tires, or plastic or wooden blocks, it becomes the Board Walk.
- **A plastic sheet and a wire mesh sheet:** These are used to expose a dog to various surfaces. Sheets of three feet by six feet are appropriate.
- **Six tires:** You can place the tires either close together, or with spaces in between,

*It can be helpful to use a little treat to reward a dog who is at first shy or fearful about trying the Board Walk.*

depending on how well your dog handles these obstacles.
- **A ladder:** Use a regular ladder made of wood or aluminum.
- **Six cones:** Cones can be used to set up the Slalom for a dog to walk through. Consider an irregular pattern for the cones as well, to give more variety and help a dog that pulls or is unfocused to listen to your signals for where to go next.

*Poles are set up at different heights to get the dog's attention and challenge him to use his body in a new way. The red section draws his attention to the middle of the poles.*

*The Star can be set up with the poles at different distances. Generally, you want the farthest distance to be about the length of your dog.*

*Mats of different material and a grid are useful when teaching your dog to walk on different surfaces.*

## Safety Tips

- It is important that all obstacles are constructed safely. Watch out for movable parts, sharp edges, and splinters.
- Be careful when working with a dog that is aggressive toward other dogs. Keep a sufficient distance.
- Lead a difficult dog in the Journey of the Homing Pigeon (with another person). He will be easier to control, and consequently learn faster (p. 106).

*Jolly and I are working on the Ladder. I am using motivating body language to support the dog.*

# The Labyrinth

Leading the dog through the Labyrinth is useful in many aspects. The boundaries created by the boards or poles teach the dog to concentrate on his handler, and listen to the smallest signals given to him through the leash, voice and your body language.

## HOW TO

**1 Leading** This is the first time Shawnee is wearing the Holt and she needs to learn to accept the new sensation on her face. Robyn takes her through the Labyrinth to give her something else to think about. You can see how Robyn holds her hands at different levels. Both leashes are loose and Robyn's body is turned toward her dog.

**2 Turning** Robyn turns her upper body into Shawnee's direction so she can keep an eye on her. She is using body language in addition to a take-and-release on the leash to influence the dog's speed. Robyn steps ahead of Shawnee and brings her right hand forward ahead of the dog's nose. She indicates the turn with her right hand and by turning her body in the direction she wants her dog to go. The dog should be in the middle of the Labyrinth so she does not feel crowded.

# WHAT IT LOOKS LIKE

The Labyrinth gives the dog a visual boundary so he can change his habits and behavior patterns when being led, and it is a fun way for the dog to learn something new. Every time you expose your dog to a new pattern of movement, his ability to learn is increased.

1 Shawnee lunges at Tess as the two dogs are led through the Labyrinth. Robyn is turning Shawnee's head with the Holt and is pulling Shawnee toward her with the leash attached to the collar.

2 This time Robyn places herself between the dogs. Shawnee is watching Tess nervously, and is ready to lunge. The Holt with the double leash helps Robyn control Shawnee.

3 After several practice runs I stay in one place with Tess while Robyn walks toward us. Note that both Robyn and I are positioned between the dogs.

4 Robyn allows Shawnee to look in Tess' direction as long as Shawnee stays calm. At the same time, I stroke Shawnee with a Wand to calm her and establish contact. Tess is helping by using "calming signals" to settle Shawnee.

# The Boards

One of the most effective obstacles to influence your dog's physical and emotional balance is the Boards. Place three solid, wooden boards about one foot wide and ten feet long in the shape of a "V" or "Y" on the ground. Only use this configuration in the beginning until the dog is comfortable and feels confident about walking on the narrow board.

## HOW TO

**1–4 Three Boards**  Quivive is unsure about walking on the slippery surface of the Boards. She hesitates as soon as she steps on the first one. When Boards are placed in the shape of a "Y" it is easier for a dog to find the entrance and understand the intention of the obstacle. Gabi can easily influence her dog by having the Balance Leash in both hands. It is important to hold the leash between your thumb and index finger so you can stay light and softly influence the dog.

Stop just before the obstacle so your dog gets a chance to think and find his mental and emotional balance

Quivive made some impressive changes with this obstacle as you can see by the way she is quietly standing in this last photo.

## What should you do if...
### ...your dog jumps off the Board?

One solution is to place an optical barrier beside the Boards, such as brightly colored poles. Two poles can also act as a helpful guide when placed in the "V" shape or like an aisle to point out the way to the obstacle. If your dog steps off the Board, calmly take him back and try again. Be sure to work slowly, take the dog one step at a time and stay level with his head. Remember to let him have fun; praise with your voice as well as some TTouches. If your dog is shy, timid or fearful offer him a little treat, but don't lure him onto the Boards.

# Wire Mesh and Plastic Surfaces

Leading your dog over a Wire Mesh Screen, or a Plastic Surface, is a good way to train him to follow you onto any unusual or slippery surfaces. It is also an important exercise in the training of Therapy and Search-and-Rescue dogs that have to walk securely, and without fear, on any surface. For an unusual surface, use fine-gauge, window-screen material and staple it to a frame. Any kind of hard plastic that does not splinter can be used to simulate an icy surface.

## HOW TO

If your dog gets nervous when working with obstacles and tenses his paws, I recommend preparing him with Coiled Python TTouches on the legs and Raccoon TTouches on the pads of the paws. This way you can get his attention as well as build a new connection to the ground. When a dog is nervous, his muscles get tense and this restricts the circulation in the legs. You can also put a Body Wrap on him to give him more security and stability. You can encourage the dog by placing some food on the obstacle. The more unusual walking surfaces you can offer your dog, the more trusting and self-confident he will be in all new situations.

## WHAT IT LOOKS LIKE

1 I am using an ordinary leash on Jesse for the first time over the fine wire screen attached to a thick frame. Jesse is walking slowly and placing her feet carefully. I am encouraging her with my voice and praising her for successfully trying to negotiate the obstacle.

2 Young dogs learn much more quickly being led from both sides over an obstacle. Using both hands, Kirsten is leading T-Rex with a lead attached to both the collar and a Holt, while I am further away and just using a regular leash attached to the collar, and a Wand. The leashes are in a neutral position so that the dog is free to investigate the surface.

3 Chablis, a Collie, is being led in the Journey of the Homing Pigeon. The leashes have two points of contact (harness and flat collar). Ideally, the leashes should not be attached to the same rings.

4 Angelika leads Giacomo over the Plastic Surface to the Wire Mesh. This is asking quite a lot of the poodle; the obstacle could be made easier by providing more space between each surface.

## What should you do if...
### ...you don't have access to a Playground for Higher Learning?

The obstacles that we use are as simple as possible. You can make them from materials you already have around the house. You really do not need a professional training course with these particular obstacles. Tellington Method obstacles can be set up quickly in your backyard, or in a parking lot. You can use an ordinary large sheet of plastic to simulate a slippery surface, and mesh window screen for the wire surface.

Walking around trees, up and down off a curb, or starting and stopping on a hill can all be things you can use on a walk to gain some of the benefit of the Playground.

For self-assurance and confidence

# The Teeter-Totter (Seesaw)

The Teeter-Totter is an obstacle especially suited for improving your dog's balance and sure-footedness. He will learn to trust you in any situation even when something unexpected happens. Start with a very low Teeter-Totter (four inches high) and control the tipping of the board with your foot when you begin.

## HOW TO

1  Stop in front of the Teeter-Totter and lightly tap the board with your Wand to call your dog's attention to the obstacle. Gimli is following Jo's wand as she walks next to Gimli's head. This Teeter-Totter is very low to give the dog the chance to master the obstacle one step at a time and learn to find the tipping point. He needs to stay confident when the board tips so Jo helps him by controlling the movement of the board with her foot. Watch my DVD, *Unleash Your Dog's Potential* (www.ttouch.com) to see the steps.

2  Gimli had no problem when the Teeter-Totter tipped, but now there is a misunderstanding. Using the Wand, Jo thwarts Gimli's attempt to get off the board before finishing the exercise. The mistake occurred because Jo was standing too far back and forgot that Gimli was supposed to follow the Wand.

# What should you do if...
#### ....the dog jumps off the Teeter-Totter?

Simplify the obstacle. Use a wide board and a smaller block. Put some food on the board to encourage your dog to walk slowly. Take your time and proceed slowly, step by step. If your dog jumps off, or does not walk in a straight line, try using a Holt and, perhaps, the "Suitcase" (p. 95). Make sure you stay at the dog's head when leading him.

## WHAT IT LOOKS LIKE

**1** Jesse walked along this board on the ground before it was put on the tire to make a Teeter-Totter. Now, she is watching as a helper puts some food on the obstacle to encourage her to walk on it again.

**2** I put the board on the tire balanced in such a way so that one end cannot tip. I lead Jesse with a rope that I've placed around her chest right behind her shoulder. This helps me to control direction.

**3** I stop Jesse as the board tips down. I am supporting her by her collar and the chest ring so that she waits calmly.

**4** We raise the Teeter-Totter to make it lighter. I am putting my weight on the board to tip it down slowly while Jesse stands in the middle getting used to the motion.

## For balance, agility and confidence

# The Board Walk

The Board Walk builds confidence and is excellent preparation for agility and other dog sports. Apart from the fun you and your dog can have, this exercise improves the dog's agility, balance and self-confidence. The low Board Walk is a good preparation for the A-Frame, Teeter-Totter and raised Board Walk for potential agility dogs. The dog will learn to effortlessly walk on a narrow board without falling off. You can use car tires, and plastic or wooden blocks to raise the platform.

## HOW TO

In Photo 4, I am demonstrating the simplest form of the Board Walk, which can create amazing results. By raising the obstacle and making it more difficult, dogs can gain valuable experience that enhances their trust in you and confidence in themselves. Use a Balance Leash, harness or head halter when your dog has a tendency to rush. Your goal is to get the dog to walk slowly and with increased awareness. Stop your dog in the middle of the obstacle if he rushes.

Before asking more of him, consider his age, health and breed. Note: Dogs with ailments of the spine, hip dysplasia or arthritis should not be taken over the A-Frame or raised Board Walk.

## WHAT IT LOOKS LIKE

**1–2 Leading with the Balance Leash and Head Halter** Gabi is leading her dog with the Balance Leash in Photo 1, and with the head halter in Photo 2 using both hands. You can see that Quivive is still trying to find her balance in the first picture. Gabi holds the leash between her thumb and index finger so she can give very light, precise signals. On their second try, wearing the head halter (Photo 2), Gabi no longer needs to support her dog and Quivive is walking in balance and confidently along the plank.

**3 Leading with the Harness** With his dog wearing a harness, Dirk takes his strong Labrador across the Board Walk. Dirk has two hands on the leash, which is loose. The dog is paying attention and walking in good balance.

**4 Leading with Just One Hand** Using just one hand, I am showing how to lead the dog who is wearing a harness. As soon as the dog has gained confidence, he will be able to master this obstacle independently—without a person helping.

# Poles, Cavalletti and the Star

Exercises with Poles, Cavalletti, and the Star will improve your dog's concentration, focus, and agility. He learns to move with awareness. Poles are also good training for improving the gait and fitness of show dogs, and for preparing dogs for agility classes.

## WHAT IT LOOKS LIKE

**1–2 Poles**  I am leading Grey over unevenly raised poles. Holes in the cones allow us to raise the ends to different heights. The red paint on the poles indicates their middle section. I am also walking over the poles to show the dog what to do. Once he is familiar with the obstacle, I will walk beside it.

**3 Cavalletti**  Jo is leading Gimli over six cavalletti. Gimli jogs over the center of the poles while Jo walks next to the cavalletti showing Gimli the way with her Wand. This exercise is used to improve a dog's gait and lightness of movement.

 **4 The Star**  Gimli is following Jo's Wand through the Star which here, consists of six poles. Gimli is walking on the inside, which is more difficult than the outside, because the poles are higher and closer together. This is an excellent exercise for improving general coordination.

1

## What should you do if ...
### ...the dog participates but with no enjoyment?

Make sure you praise your dog for each success. If you are enjoying yourself and having fun, your dog will probably feel the same. Also, consider inviting friends and their dogs so that you can all work together. Making training a social event will probably motivate both you and your dog.

3

2

4

# The Ladder and Tires

The Ladder and the Tires exercises are a challenge for some dogs. The different materials and shapes of these objects provide new experiences. Each exercise influences a dog in a way that cannot be predicted. For the Ladder exercise, put a simple ladder on the ground. For the Tires, use four to eight tires, and place them in various configurations. The object is to create challenges that will develop a dog's confidence in dealing with new, and unusual, situations.

## HOW TO

When working the Ladder your dog must pay close attention to what he is doing and adjust the length of his stride to the distance between the rungs. If your dog is afraid and will not step into the spaces between the rungs, walk him across the width of the ladder; zigzag him back and forth across the ladder several times; follow another dog; or put some treats in the spaces between the rungs. If you want to help your dog walk the entire length and he is somewhat insecure, you can place one side of the ladder next to a wall. This way you only need to control your dog on one side and he cannot step out of the ladder.

When working the Tires, your dog can start by walking on the outer edges of the Tires. Make the exercise more difficult by asking him to step into the center of the Tires. Some dogs will be encouraged if you drop treats into the middle of them.

## WHAT IT LOOKS LIKE

**1 Leading with the Wand**  I am leading Tess with a simple leash attached to her collar and with the Wand across the ladder. Tess is attentive and is lowering her head as she walks through the obstacle.

**2–3 Leading with the Harness**  Angelika leads Eddie over the ladder using two hands. He is concerned and she drops treats between each bar. This motivates the dog and he eagerly looks for the next treat, keeping his head low and looking at the obstacle. At the end of the ladder, Angelika stops her dog and praises him with her voice.

**4 The Tires**  Grady, a two-year-old Standard Poodle, is being led over an obstacle for the first time. Stroking him with the Wand on his front legs helps him to calm down so that he can concentrate on the job at hand. Robyn is leading him with a Balance Leash in order to bring him into balance and stop him from forging ahead. Since Grady is nervous about walking on, or touching, the tires, they have been placed in such a way so there is a space between the rows. This simplifies the obstacle. The goal is for the dog to be successful, so make the obstacles easy in the beginning, working up to more difficult challenges. In this way, you can start him off walking between the tires. The objective is to get the dog to walk along the rims, and then into the middle of the tires themselves.

## For more flexibility

# The Slalom with Cones

Focus and flexibility are emphasized in the Slalom made up of cones. This is another obstacle that you may know from regular dog-agility training. It is great fun for both dogs and humans. At first, practice the Slalom with a leash and at slow speed. Once your dog understands what he is supposed to do, you can speed up, and finally even discard the leash. You need five or six cones set up in a straight line. When you start, the distance between the cones should be at least as long as the dog's body.

### HOW TO

**1–2 Off Leash Around the Cones** Tess is running through the cones without a leash. I am directing her with hand signals and body language. She is cooperating well and is running in tight curves around the cones while watching my right hand. Sometimes, you may find it helpful to use treats to motivate a dog to do this exercise.

If you keep your training sessions short you will find that your dog processes what he has learned between sessions, and he will be more skilled the next time.

## WHAT IT LOOKS LIKE

**1** Shawnee is wearing a Holt and a Body Wrap to gain confidence. Robyn is walking ahead of her dog to show her the way and using both hands on the leash to guide Shawnee through the cones. Her left hand, which is in front, indicates the direction she wants Shawnee to turn, and her right hand, which is further back, helps to regulate the speed.

**2** Robyn's clear signals on the leash emphasize the turn. Shawnee must learn to stay as close to the cones as possible in order to negotiate them smoothly and quickly.

**3** Concentration is important for the Slalom. Practice walking through the Slalom course in both directions, and lead the dog from both sides. As a result, both of you will become more flexible.

### What should you do if...
...the dog skips a cone?

Increase the space between the cones because the dog may be finding tight turns difficult. If so, check to see if the dog has a physical problem that makes turning hard for him. If not, it could be a lack of flexibility or focus. It can also be helpful to follow another team through the cones, and do some TTouches to increase mobility and balance.

# Appendices

# Checklist

Many typical unwanted behaviors can be changed with the Tellington Method. This checklist will make it easier for you to find the solution to change your dog's health or behavior. Of course, TTouch never replaces a visit to your veterinarian, but can be used during the trip to the vet, prevent some ailments and support any ongoing treatment by your veterinarian.

| For your dog | |
| --- | --- |
| Fear of strangers or the veterinarian | Ear TTouch, Lying Leopard TTouch |
| Fear of loud noises | Tail TTouch, Mouth TTouch, Body Wrap, Ear TTouch |
| Urinating due to fear or excitement | Ear TTouch, Tiger TTouch |
| Uncontrollable barking | Head Halter, Ear TTouch, Lying Leopard TTouch, Mouth TTouch, Ear TTouch |
| Hyperactivity | Coiled Python TTouch, Clouded Leopard TTouch, Zigzag TTouch, Body Wrap, Head Halter, Ear TTouch |
| Performance anxiety | Ear TTouch, Mouth TTouch, Coiled Python TTouch, Lick of the Cow's Tongue |
| Fear and insecurity | Ear TTouch, Mouth TTouch, Leg Circles, Tail TTouch, Body Wrap, Clouded Leopard TTouch |
| Shyness | Lying Leopard TTouch, Tail TTouch, Body Wrap |
| Chewing | Mouth TTouch |
| Aggression toward dogs | Head Halter, Clouded Leopard TTouch, Body Wrap, Leading exercises with other dogs |
| Aggression toward cats | Head Halter, TTouches in the presence of a cat, Body Wrap |
| Leash-Pulling | Head Halter, Balance Leash, Obstacles, Clouded Leopard TTouch |
| Dragging on leash | Head Halter, Body Wrap, Ear TTouch, Python TTouch, Leg Circles |
| Car sickness | Ear TTouch |
| Restlessness in the car | Ear TTouch, Head Halter, Body Wrap |
| Problems being brushed | Tarantulas Pulling the Plow, Hair Slides, TTouch with a sheepskin, Coiled Python TTouch |
| Problems being bathed | Ear TTouch, Coiled Python TTouch, Hair Slides, Leg Circles before and during the bath |
| Problems with nail clipping | Python TTouch on the legs, Raccoon TTouch on the paws and nails, Leg Circles, TTouch with the paws |

| After acute injury | On the way to the vet: Ear TTouch, light Raccoon TTouch on the entire body except the injured area |
|---|---|
| Scars | Raccoon TTouch, Lying Leopard TTouch |
| Before surgery | Ear TTouch, Lying Leopard TTouch |
| Fever | On the way to the vet: Ear TTouch |
| Shock after an accident | On the way to the vet: Ear TTouch, then Lying Leopard TTouch |
| Arthritis | Python TTouch, Raccoon TTouch, Ear TTouch, Body Wrap |
| Hip problems | Daily Raccoon TTouch, Python TTouch, Tail TTouch |
| Teething | Mouth TTouch with a cold washcloth |
| Digestive disorders | Ear TTouch, Belly Lifts, Lying Leopard on the belly |
| Stomachaches | On the way to the vet: Ear TTouch, Belly Lifts |
| Sensitive ears | Llama TTouch, Lying Leopard TTouch with a sheepskin, circles on the ears close to the body while supporting the head |
| Sore muscles | Python TTouch, Coiled Python TTouch |
| Problem getting up or climbing stairs | Body Wrap, Belly Lifts, Python TTouch, Tarantulas Pulling the Plow, Tail TTouch, Ear TTouch, Lick of the Cow's Tongue |
| Allergies | Bear TTouch, Ear TTouch, Clouded Leopard TTouch |
| Itchiness | Tiger TTouch, Bear TTouch with a washcloth |
| **For the female** | |
| Pregnancy | Belly Lifts, Lying Leopard TTouch and Coiled Python TTouch on the belly, Raccoon TTouch, Ear TTouch |
| Support during birth | Ear TTouch, Lying Leopard TTouch, Python TTouch, Coiled Python TTouch |
| Rejecting the puppies | Ear TTouch, Lying Leopard TTouch with a warm washcloth on the nipples, Mouth TTouch |
| Problems conceiving | Ear TTouch, Tail TTouch, Coiled Python TTouch on the hind end, Clouded Leopard TTouch |
| **For the male** | |
| Aggression toward male dogs | Head Halter, Labyrinth, Wand, leading with other dogs, Journey of the Homing Pigeon, neutering |
| **For your puppy** | |
| Teething | Mouth TTouch |
| Refusing to nurse | Mouth TTouch, Ear TTouch, light TTouches on the tongue, Raccoon TTouch on the entire body |
| Socializing | Mouth TTouch, Ear TTouch, Clouded Leopard TTouch, Tail TTouch, TTouch on the paws |
| Nail trimming | Python TTouch on the legs, Raccoon TTouch on the paws and nails |

# To contact Tellington TTouch Training

Visit www.ttouch.com for a complete list
of offices and TTouch Instructors around
the world.

## TTEAM and TTouch in the US

1713 State Road 502
Santa Fe, NM 87506
866.488.6824
info@ttouch.com

## TTEAM and TTouch in Canada

5435 Rochdell Road
Vernon, BC V1B 3E8
250.545.2336
www.tteam-ttouch.ca

## TTEAM and TTouch in the UK

www.ttouchtteam.co.uk

## TTEAM and TTouch in Australia

www.ttouchaustralia.com.au

*This book is dedicated to my sister, Robyn Hood, who has TTouched the lives of so many people and their dogs.*

## Acknowledgments

Many people have contributed to the preparation of this book and its translation from German into English, for which I am most grateful. My first thanks goes to Caroline Robbins, my American publisher, who was incredibly supportive and spent endless hours editing and working with me on parts of the book. Thank you, Caroline, for your patience and dedication.

And thank you, Christine Schwartz for your dedication to the translation of the book into English, and to Kirsten Henry for filling in the spaces (when Caroline could not find me in Europe!) Debby Potts gets huge accolades for late-night editing after her classes in Germany, often working into the wee hours of the morning. Thank you Rebecca Didier for the final edits to this book.

My heartfelt thanks to Gudrun Braun, who had the original vision for the first edition of this book, and who is responsible for the layout, photo shoot, and organization of this second edition in German. Thank you to Karin Freiling for working with me on the section on stress, and Kathy Cascade for her contribution to the section on calming signals. And thanks to Gabi

Maue, Bibi Degn and Karin Freiling for assisting Gudrun in the editorial process.

Thanks to my sister, Robyn Hood, for her years of support of the development of Tellington TTouch; teaching TTouch around the globe; and editing an international Tellington TTouch and TTEAM newsletter since 1984!

It was my wish to include words of wisdom from some of our most experienced instructors and practitoners in this second edition: My thanks to Edie Jane Eaton and Debby Potts for taking TTouch to New Zealand and Japan; and for the skillful teaching of Kathy Cascade, Bibi Degn, Karin Freiling, and Katja Krauss for all the dogs, cats, and small critters (and their people) whose lives they have enriched. My deepest gratitude to Daniela Zurr and Martina Simmerer for their reports on the experience of TTouch in their veterinary practices,

It was also a great experience shooting the new photos with Gabi Metz and her partner Marc Heppner. Thanks to you both.

I thank Karin Freiling, Gabi Maue, and Lisa Leicht for their help at the photo shoot, and Hella Koss for organizing it. Another huge thank you to Dirk Koss, Renate Janisch, Sylvia Osswald, Angelika Stahl, Irmgard Mende, and Brigitte Wigand, for bringing their dogs.

Cornelia Koller did an outstanding job on the illustrations.

I also want to thank my Kosmos publisher, Almuth Sieben, for her support of my work over two decades.

Thanks to Kirsten Henry, Carol Lang, Judy Spoonhoward, and Holly Sanchez for keeping our office in New Mexico running so smoothly.

My thanks to the organizers of TTouch trainings around the world, including TTouch Instructors Sarah Fisher and Tina Constance in the UK; Eugenie Chopin in South Africa; Lisa Leicht and Teresa Cotarelli-Gunter in Switzerland; Valeria Boissier in Italy; Sylvia Haveman and Monique Staring in Holland; Martin Lasser and Doris Prisinger in Austria; Debby Potts and Lauren McCall in Japan.

Thanks to my husband, Roland Kleger, for his willingness to keep me company no matter how late I stay up writing, and for his countless hours of excellent editing. Like all of us who teach this work around the world, Roland is dedicated to Changing the World One TTouch at a Time.

# Index